97 THINGS TO DO Before You Finish HIGH SCHOOL

First published in 2007 by Zest Books
35 Stillman Street, Suite 121, San Francisco, CA 94107
www.zestbooks.net

Created and produced by Zest Books, San Francisco, CA
© 2007, 2011 by Zest Books
Illustrations © 2007 by Azadeh Houshyar

Text set in Sabon; title text set in Bureau Agency and Triplex

Library of Congress Control Number: 2007928299
ISBN-13: 978-0-9790173-0-8
ISBN-10: 0-9790173-0-0

CREDITS
EDITORIAL DIRECTOR/BOOK EDITOR: Karen Macklin
CREATIVE DIRECTOR: Hallie Warshaw
ILLUSTRATOR: Azadeh Houshyar
GRAPHIC DESIGNERS: Tanya Napier and Cari McLaughlin
PRODUCTION ARTIST: Cari McLaughlin
TEEN ADVISORY BOARD: Carolyn Hou, Diana Kozlova, Maxfield J. Peterson, Joe Pinsker, Hannah Shr

Manufactured in China
LEO 10 9 8 7 6 5 4 3
4500397654

Every effort has been made to ensure that the information presented is accurate. The publisher disclaims any liability for injuries, losses, untoward results, or any other damages that may result from the use of the information in this book.

97 THINGS TO DO Before You Finish HIGH SCHOOL

Steven Jenkins and Erika Stalder

Illustrations by Azadeh Houshyar

This is the best time of your life — or so people keep telling you. But then, those same people tell you to clean your room, be home before 10, work on the weekends, and hand in 20-page research papers. Uh, OK.

Whether or not *you* think this is the best time of your life (and the truth is, for most people, it keeps getting better), it *is* a unique time. As a teenager, you have the capacity to learn anything you want at a speed much faster than people who are only five years older, and your curiosity and insightfulness are at an all-time high.

So, what to do? Well, you can't stop doing the things you *have* to do. School, home, family: These are all aspects of basic life maintenance. But how you spend your free time—well, that's a different story. This book is about all of the things they don't teach you at home or in class, like the right way to throw a party, how to take a killer road trip, the best ways to get your bod in shape, and how to protect the environment (better than your parents did). 97 *Things* also includes great stuff to do that is off the beaten path, like DJing, writing your own manifesto, and even understanding the stock market.

There is a lot in here, and clearly you don't have to do it *all*. Pick and choose what speaks to you. Go chronologically or flip through. Read the book alone and set goals, or page through it with friends and make plans to do stuff together. Most important, use it to get ideas about how you want to spend your time and who you want to be. Because you're only young once … and it happens to be now.

97 Things To Do ...

ONE: For Your Personal Development [14]

TWO: With/For Friends [40]

97 Things To Do ...

THREE: With/For Family [60]

FOUR: For Your Body [76]

97 Things To Do ...

SIX: To Express Yourself [110]

SEVEN: To Benefit Your Community and Environment [142]

97 Things To Do ...

EIGHT: Because You Should [162]

NINE: Because You're Only Young Once [188]

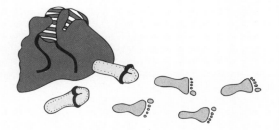

1 Redo Your Bedroom

Face it—your bedroom is the only place you can call your own. It should reflect your ideology, personality, and charm. But who chose the furniture, wallpaper, and paint? Were these stylistic atrocities forced on you by clueless decorators whose ideas of cool were ballerina figurines and tiger-striped throw pillows? Reclaim this precious space by redecorating. All it takes to transform your bedroom is some ingenuity and a little (very little) cash. Even if a complete overhaul isn't possible right now, you can style your space with personal touches to make it unmistakably yours.

How to Do It

1. First, clean up. It's a drag, but that's the only way to get a good look at the space. To redesign, you need some room to experiment. Free up space by moving out things you no longer want or need. (Keep your "out pile" around until you are totally finished because you may re-use that stuff for other purposes.)

2. Once you have a partially blank slate, start putting your stamp on your stomping grounds. Think about who you are, and make your design reflect that person. If you're a sports nut, pick out memorabilia from your favorite team. Music lovers can frame old record albums and create a grid of classic covers. Maps of the world and a cool collection of international postcards work for travel lovers and adventure seekers.

3. After redecorating, revisit the stuff you took out. Can you do something to wake up that old bookshelf or nightstand? Try throwing colorful fabrics on chipped tabletops, or sanding and staining old furniture to make it look new.

4. When you're done, responsibly throw away, donate, sell, or recycle whatever you can't use.

Now, your room is your own personal creative space and the refuge from the outside world that it is supposed to be!

An Exercise in Compromise

If you share a room with a brother or sister, one option is to join forces and come up with a decorating plan that both of you can live with. But if compromise is impossible (you're all about death metal and your sib's got a thing for pink, or vice versa), just concentrate on making your half of the room a space you can truly call your own.

2 Start a Collection

Does the term "collector" bring to mind that weird old lady down the street whose house is overflowing with old phonebooks, vintage cat toys, and dustballs galore? Her collections may be an overgrown mess, but don't let that deter you from starting your own. Collections can actually be cool—if they are artful and well-maintained. It's really just a way to surround yourself with the things you love. And, if those things increase in value as time goes by, they can turn into an excellent investment. Original Natas skateboard decks from the '80s now sell for thousands of dollars, and classic Barbie dolls pull in hundreds. Whether you're into lunch boxes, snow globes, or random things with penguins on them, building a collection will send you on a rewarding quest that can never be completed. Of course, completion is not the point. The fun is in the endless search for those last three *Buffy the Vampire Slayer* action figures missing from the lineup on your desk.

How to Do It

Begin by surveying your possessions—if you have three or more of a certain type of object, you already have the makings of a collection. Do some investigating. What about a drawer filled with classic Hello Kitty stationery or that box full of original *Hellboy* comic books? Make sure you go with something you love that's both accessible and affordable. Mint-condition LPs from legendary indie labels like Rawkus Records or Sub Pop will feed your music fix and look great framed and hung on the wall. Old-school video game accessories and vintage jeans make for both quirky and functional collections, as do items from nature such as abalone shells (which can double as jewelry holders). When starting any collection, consider space—you don't want to gather a ton of musical instruments and then realize you have no room to store them. And be selective. If that Mavericks cap isn't in pristine condition, hold out for one that is. Keeping high standards will keep your collections streamlined—which will keep you from ending up like that lady down the street.

Online Buying

If you haven't yet been sucked into eBay, check it out for items to add to your collection. But keep in mind:

- Before buying, check the seller's feedback to ensure they have a track record of delivering the goods (don't deal with anyone who has racked up negative comments from buyers).

- When paying, never use a personal check. PayPal is best because it can provide buyer protection if a product never arrives or arrives busted.

- Always check the shipping rates to be sure you're not being charged too much.

3 Create a Journal

Documenting your daily ups and downs is a great outlet for frustration, confusion, and secret crushes. In the midst of all the drama, take time each day to reflect on the highs and lows of your ever-changing life. Granted, there's plenty going on these days that you'd rather forget than remember, but years from now you'll be glad you recorded high school-era high points and horrors for posterity. Was Ms. Whoever a complete troll today? Did you bomb tryouts for the team? Is your sister possibly *the* most annoying person on the planet? Write it all down. All of this will seem funny one day. Really.

How to Do It

Fill the pages of a diary with anything and everything you're thinking and feeling. There are no rules to follow—you can write long entries covering every detail of your day, or just make lists of things that drive you crazy. Write poems or confess first (or second or third) loves, record your little (and not so little) white lies. The journal is for your eyes only, so ensure privacy by keeping it locked or in a hiding place. If you're fortunate enough to have your own computer, consider keeping an online journal that mixes your textual expression with photos, illustrations, and video clips. Protect your private thoughts and images with a password. (And it doesn't hurt to have a biometric fingerprint reader enabled for extra security.)

Blog About It

If you don't already have your own blog (and, no, MySpace doesn't count), it's really easy to start one. Go to *www.blogger.com* or *www.wordpress.com* and follow the straightforward tutorials to create an account, name your blog, and set up a template. Creating posts is unbelievably simple (no HTML knowledge needed). Now your triumphs, tragedies, and innermost desires will be made public for the whole world to follow!

Of course, there is a downfall: Privacy is pretty much out the window. Learn how to use different settings or services (like Vox) for controlling who can and cannot have access to your blog. And never post personal identification information—people can and will lift your home address, phone number, and email address to stalk you, commit identity theft, or try other creepy stuff.

4 Assemble a Photo Album

Documenting dysfunctional family trips, out-of-control birthday parties, and your younger sister's sorry attempt to cut bangs is tons of fun, but what good are photos if no one ever sees them? It's time to do something with the thousands of pictures you've taken over the years. Even if every photo you've ever taken is saved on your hard drive, not a single one is accessible to the public for viewing. Real, physical, holdable photo albums are great because you can carry them with you and tell stories while people are looking at them—instead of staring at a screen. Before taking even one more snapshot, take some time to organize your Kodak (or Sony or Nikon) moments in a book.

How to Do It

To release your photos from the confines of your hard drive and share them with family and friends, log in to a site like Shutterfly, Snapfish, or Webshots and upload your photos. Choose pics that cover a time frame (summer '07), event (prom), or group of friends (your renegade fixed-gear bike crew). Order the most flattering prints—they should cost 10 to 15 cents each and arrive in the mail a few days later. Buy a classic photo album and insert your photos. The easiest ones are those with photo slots in plastic sleeves because you just pop the shots in. You can also get the kind with blank pages and insert photos into those little black corner adhesives—this style is better for adding captions.

Spending time with photos not only helps you get them in order but also makes for a great way to revisit the events you are chronicling and reflect on the good 'ol times.

Last-Minute Prezzie

Forgot to get a gift in time for Mother's Day, your good friend's birthday, or your cousin's quinceañera? Give a card letting the guest of honor know their gift is being custom made. Then, photograph the event and assemble the photo album the following day. You can quickly create an album online through most photo sites and have it shipped directly to the recipient as a complete book. When taking pictures, be sure to shoot more than just the people—details like that bikini-clad supermodel cake, over-the-top flower arrangements, or the dog's unexpected splash into the pool will help capture the feeling of the entire event and make your album an irreplaceable gift.

5 Listen to New Music

When it comes to music, you have your faves. Maybe you're a sucker for trip-hop or reggaeton, or a die-hard fan of country blues or hard rock. But as the adage goes, you don't know what you're missing till you try it. Next time you're looking for tunes, venture outside your auditory box. Download a few R&B classics, or some Latin jazz or dub-heavy reggae. New musical genres are often stylized variations of older ones. The roots of house music are steeped in disco, and the beginnings of rock emerged from gospel, so by going outside your usual genres, you're likely to find similar rhythms and styles that surprisingly rock your world.

How to Do It

Start with the type of music you love and trace its roots. If you're a hip-hop fanatic, seek out the songs Nas is sampling from—maybe classic R&B hits. If balladeers like P!nk and Christina Aguilera fill your iTunes, check out old soul or bluegrass singers. Chances are, the same chords, notes, and progressions that you dig in your modern collection will be just as prevalent in related genres. Or raid your parents' music collection and find out what was so hot about Jimi Hendrix (rock), The Cure (pop/rock), Leonard Cohen (folk), LL Cool J (rap), and Billie Holiday (jazz). You can also check out your friends' social networking pages and visit artist websites to download free MP3s of songs and styles you've never heard. If you feel like you have "discovered" a new genre, share it with a friend; rockabilly's always more fun to sing aloud to with someone else.

Can't-Miss Classics

Spin the following landmark albums that represent the best of these artists' signature styles:

- *Kind of Blue*—ultra-cool jazz masterpiece by Miles Davis

- *Cello Suites*—Bach's classically perfect six solo works

- *Revolver*—perfect pop/rock songs in every conceivable style by The Beatles

- *12 Greatest Hits*—torch and twang treasures from country queen Patsy Cline

- *The Girl From Ipanema*—sultry Brazilian singer Astrud Gilberto's smooth samba treat

- *In the Wee Small Hours*—Frank Sinatra's timeless ode to late-night heartbreak

6 Give Technology a Break

American teens spend an average of four hours a day staring at TV and computer screens, and log another few hours fiddling with handheld video games, digital music players, cell phones, and PDAs. As part of the most technologically dependent generation in history, you're hooked up, plugged in, and turned on most of your waking hours. That's cool, as long as all these images and gizmos are enriching your life. But machines can zap your soul if you rely on them too much. To end high-tech domination, put your gadgets aside and live off the grid for a weekend.

How to Do It

Finish up your channel surfing, emailing, downloading, and texting on Friday evening in preparation for two full days of tech-free bliss. Announce your plan to family and friends—they'll hold you accountable should you cave in after a few hours and check for text messages or sneak a peek at VH1. What to do with all this newfound free time? Spend the weekend reading a new book, writing in your journal, and taking walks around the neighborhood or through a nearby park. Break out the watercolors or practice yoga poses. Take a nap. And don't forget to enjoy some in-person quality time with friends or relatives you usually only instant-message with—they'll be thrilled to see your actual expressions, not just emoticons. It's crazy how much longer the days seem when you're not spending hours online, isn't it? Come Monday morning you'll feel refreshed and ready to dive back into the digital world.

Tech-Free Scheduling

Be sure to plan your no-tech weekend for a time when your schedule is actually clear. Living without a cell phone while shuttling from basketball practice to work to a party just isn't going to happen. And your English teacher probably won't take "I was having a no-tech weekend" as an excuse for turning in a handwritten paper.

25

7 Look Closely at a Work of Art

School field trips to museums make looking at art seem like work. After all, they typically amount to some boring tour guide rattling off what sounds like a lot of useless information as your teacher shushes your chatty classmates and you fantasize about lunch. That's because it is *really* hard to appreciate art in a group. If you want meaningful interaction with a work of art, go to a local museum or gallery alone or with one close friend or family member—someone who can appreciate the experience with you and share thoughts and feelings about the works on display.

How to Do It

To start, randomly roam around until you find a painting, sculpture, photograph, or installation that's got the "wow" factor—a certain something that stops you in your tracks and appeals to your senses. Study it closely to figure out how and why it moves you. Consider the artist's intention: Is he or she reflecting a deeply personal perspective or perhaps commenting on historical events or political turmoil? What do you think the artist was thinking while working on this piece? Let your mind drift as you gaze at your new favorite artwork—you'll be surprised at where it takes you. Focus on various aspects of the work, including the artist's use of color, shape, lighting, and symbolism (sure, at first it just looks like some naked chick, but maybe that nude figure represents power or freedom). If you find yourself drawn to different pieces by the same artist, get more info on that person; understanding an artist's life and history helps to better understand the work. Viewing art on a regular basis encourages you to look at the world differently, opening you up to colors, lines, and hidden meanings that can be found in lots of stuff in everyday life.

Take It With You

Flash photography is usually not permitted in museum galleries, but ask a guard if you can snap a pic without the flash, or look for a reproduction of your fave work on a postcard in the gift shop. If you go to the museum regularly, you can build up a collection of these postcards and put them into a small, funky photo album or make a mosaic out of them on your bedroom wall.

8 Attend a Theater Performance

If you think theater is dry or stuffy, think again. Theater is an arena for expression, and that means pretty much anything goes. Even in Shakespeare's day, there was scandal and intrigue on the stage, with power-hungry characters going all homicidal, affairs being had, and empires being lost. (Shakespeare, when you break it down, is actually pretty racy stuff.) Today, the great history of drama continues. In the edgy 1990s musical *Rent*, bohemian artists (mainly HIV-positive twentysomethings) struggle to make ends meet and sustain their dreams. And in the politically charged musical *Urinetown*, a water shortage leaves people having to pay to pee on a daily basis. Attending a professional performance of an epic drama (like *Hamlet* or *The Crucible*) or a scandalicious musical (like *Cabaret* or *Chicago*) can be a revelatory experience. You'll laugh, you'll cry ... you'll find out why your gay friends knew all the words to the *Dreamgirls* soundtrack way before the movie came out.

How to Do It

Check your local paper for theater listings. You could look for a well-known drama or a musical that sounds familiar—maybe a play you've read in school but haven't had a chance to see performed live. If you live in New York, Broadway is in your backyard, and there are always discounted tickets for students available. If not, Broadway-bound performances often tour throughout the country before their New York City runs, so if you're willing to take a chance on an unknown hit (or miss) you might be able to catch the next *Wicked* right in your hometown. Large regional theaters are also worth checking out and small theaters are your cheapest and least conventional bet as they like to do plays by local, up-and-coming writers and directors. The really small ones tend to do more experimental performances that include stuff your parents (and even you, too) might think is weird, but they do provide great conversation fodder.

Sixth Row, Center Aisle

Volunteer to be a theater usher. All you have to do is show patrons to their seats and point out drinking fountains and bathrooms in the lobby. In exchange, you'll get to see the play for free and maybe even meet the actors and behind-the-scenes crew at a post-performance party. Contact the theater's administrative offices to sign up.

9 Connect With a Role Model

The adults in your life, from parents and teachers to bosses and coaches, are (for better or for worse) your main authority figures. They try to teach you right from wrong and urge you to maximize your potential. They also, often, get on your nerves. Sometimes we love the adult figures in our lives, and sometimes we wish they would just go away. But that doesn't change the fact that it is important to have *some* kind of role model in your life — someone you actually look forward to spending time with and whose abilities, intelligence, and gusto drive and inspire you.

How to Do It

You probably already have a role model and don't realize it. That person might be someone you know, like a particularly gifted friend of the family, a coach, a yoga teacher, or an older cousin. It might even be a local community leader who has done much to improve your neighborhood. To connect with this person, simply ask for a bit of his or her time. If you look up to your ballet instructor, ask her if you can help set up before or clean up after class. If it's a professional photographer you want to learn from, ask him if you can assist on his next shoot. Talk to your role models about how they've gotten to where they are. What you learn from them will stay with you long after high school.

Put Into Words

Some role models are people you'll never meet—they're famous or from another time period or both. These people are still definitely worth reading up on, and many, such as Lance Armstrong, Sidney Poitier, and Maya Angelou, have even written memoirs and autobiographies. Reading these tomes is like having a revolutionary figure serve as a personal mentor, inspiring you to become the next great thing.

Flaws and All

Throughout your life, your role models will change as you do. You'll outgrow one and connect with another and eventually become a role model yourself. It's important to remember that the point of having a role model is to get inspired, not to have unrealistic expectations of a fellow human being. Don't put them on a pedestal: Even the greatest among us will make mistakes or say dumb things from time to time, just like everyone else.

10 Develop the Art of Conversation

"Hey, man, what's up?"

"I don't know, nothin'. What's up with you?"

"Juschillin'."

"OK, cool."

"Yeah, okay, cool. Later."

If this sounds like one of your recent conversations, it might be time to raise the bar a bit on your verbal ping-pong. Laconic head-nodding should not be mistaken for deeply meaningful communication. People measure us by what we say, so even if we are the most incredible, interesting, thoughtful people on the planet, it means little if we can't express it. Don't worry if the gift of gab doesn't come naturally for you. Conversation is an art, which means it takes practice.

How to Do It

So, how does one evolve out of the caveman stage of conversation? Easy: Just talk. You're an endlessly fascinating person with tons of interests, opinions, and good advice. So is whoever you're talking to—they just might not know how to express themselves yet.

Next time you're stuck in the communication dead zone, take the lead by asking questions: What did you do last weekend? What college are you thinking about going to? Which basketball team are you rooting for in tomorrow's big game? And don't accept one-word answers. Ask follow-up questions, like: What was your favorite song at the concert? Why are you interested in that college? When did you become a Knicks fan? It's all about the details. It's also fun to bond over shared concerns and complaints: too much homework, dating woes, and clueless parents. And, above all, take the "um" challenge: For one day, try substituting "um" (and overused words like "nothing" and "cool") with more creative word choices.

The Lost Art of Listening

Good conversation is about a lot more than talking. To really be able to keep a conversation running, you have to express genuine interest in what someone is telling you and truly listen. This will ensure a chat with balanced give and take, instead of one that's about you, you, you.

11 Make a Public Speech

Do you suffer from glossophobia? That's the fear of public speaking, and it's one of the most common phobias worldwide. Even the most confident person is bound to get a bit nervous when standing up in front of a crowd to pontificate on current events, Tim Burton, or the dangers of Digital Rights Management (aka DRM). At some point you're going to face a group of strangers, all of whom are intensely focused on what you're about to say. Learning to make a public speech is unnerving but ultimately very rewarding, and with a few helpful tips and plenty of practice, you can learn to captivate an audience better than the next crazed television evangelist.

Learn From the Laugh Masters

Usually, jokes are delivered in a circular pattern—they begin with a statement, tell a story to back up their stance, then revisit the original statement, which becomes the punch line. Great speeches have similar patterns. To see for yourself, study the way actors deliver their opening monologues on *Saturday Night Live* or how your favorite comedian delivers her material.

How to Do It

Do you think MLK rattled off his legendary "I Have a Dream" speech without staying up all night to prep and revise? Doubtful. The key to making a good speech is thorough preparation. That doesn't mean simply having a sheet of paper in front of you with some notes scratched on it. Use the checklist on the next page to ensure a great speech.

- **Keep it short and sweet.** Unless you've been given an allotted time for your speech that dictates otherwise, keep your talk to 20 minutes or less or you'll likely lose your audience (just think of how bored you get when your history teacher drones on and on).

- **Provide background and relative examples.** If you're talking about digital rights to a group of geezers at the senior center, be sure to break down exactly what DRM is and compare how record companies are infringing upon your rights today to how forms of censorship may have infringed upon their rights when they were young.

- **Practice, practice, practice.** Read your speech several times before debuting. You'll get to know it so well that you won't have to glance at your notes the entire time, freeing you to make all-important eye contact with audience members.

- **Use more than words.** Choose specific visuals, like colorful charts or pictures, to add visual impact.

- **Don't flatline.** Allow your tone to fluctuate to express surprise, shock, authority, and other emotions. (But don't overdo it— you're not Tyra Banks.)

You enter a room lit only by candles. Your biology teacher flies in through the window, dressed like Ozzy Ozbourne and playing Death Cab for Cutie's "I Will Follow You Into the Dark" on the banjo. A talking dog appears out of nowhere and makes fun of your haircut. You try to explain that the Titanic is about to sink in a bathtub filled with strawberry yogurt, but just then Antonio Banderas calls to remind you about tonight's prom at Disneyland. Your cell phone turns into a lobster. Just as you're about to discover the cure for boredom, you awake to the sound of your alarm clock. You're just thankful that the dream is over, but what does it all mean?

Dreams and Sex

You may have heard before that Sigmund Freud, the father of modern psychoanalysis, believed that most dreams are a representation of the dreamer's sexual desires. But that's just one man's opinion. So don't freak out if that weird kid from school shows up in your dream wearing a cheerleading uniform and talking like Stewie from *Family Guy*. It probably just means you need to watch less TV.

How to Do It

Interpreting your nighttime visions is a fascinating trip into the deep, dark secrets of the unconscious mind. To start on the journey, keep a dream journal on your nightstand, and jot down as many details as you can remember as soon as you wake up. Read over your notes and think about what each element of the dream might symbolize. Maybe your bio teacher is telling you that music, not science, is a likely career option. Did you forget to brush the dog last weekend? A-ha! And maybe you've been eating too much yogurt lately and feel like you're drowning in it. It's all beginning to make sense. As for Antonio … well, you'll have to figure that one out on your own. If your dreams are not too embarrassing, share them with your best friend and swap interpretations. You can also consult online dream dictionaries for further analysis. The most important thing is to keep an open mind and embrace the subconscious.

Bad Dreams

The occasional scary dream is totally normal, but if you're having a lot of nightmares, you should talk to someone about it. The realities of homework, chores, and curfews are stressful enough—your dreams shouldn't suck too.

13 Join a Club

Do you have guilty pleasures that your friends can't identify with? Are you addicted to *Glee*, enamored with Supergirl, or obsessed with Samuel L. Jackson? No matter how esoteric your hobby or obsession—from Wes Anderson movies to unicycles to *Battlestar Galactica*— fellow fanatics lurk nearby, eager to swap stories and out-geek you with their mastery of related trivia. If you can't beat 'em, join 'em! Sign up for a club and meet like-minded people. You may have only one thing in common, but for one night each month it'll be a blast to get together and revel in your shared love of whatever that thing is.

How to Do It

Search online for local meetups of hobby enthusiasts—type in the name of your hobby, followed by the name of your city, and see what comes up. If you're into baseball cards, model cars, or another highly popular collectible, attend a convention and discover local groups that gather regularly. Lots of bands and TV shows have periodic fan club meetings in cities across the

country, where you can good-naturedly argue about Led Zeppelin's best album or the worst *America's Next Top Model* contestant (find out about these gatherings online). Check out your local community center for activity clubs such as conversational Spanish, advanced chess, poetry writing, and tae kwon do. If you can't find a local club in your area of interest, start one yourself by posting a notice on your favorite networking site. When investigating an already established group, keep in mind some clubs are geared toward teens only, while others will mix up members of all ages and backgrounds. For those that mix ages, go with an adult to the first meeting to make sure the other members aren't creepy.

Did You Know?

Legend has it that Shakespeare was a member of the Friday Street Club, a social group that met once a month at the Mermaid Tavern in London from 1612–1613. Just imagine him complaining about writer's block with poet Sir Walter Raleigh and other Elizabethan-era scribes.

14 Host a Film Festival

Film festivals are held all over the world as glamorous showcases for Hollywood blockbusters and independent flicks. Film fests are not limited to entertainment capitals such as LA, New York, and Berlin—they happen regularly in many towns across the country. If you're a movie buff but can't yet jet-set to Cannes or hobnob with Chloë Sevigny and Johnny Depp at Sundance, it's easy to start your own festival. With carefully selected programs, a cozy screening space (like your living room), and exclusive invitations to a few lucky friends, your fest will become the can't-miss event of the season.

How to Do It

Roam the local video store or DVD rental websites like Netflix or GreenCine in search of intriguing films that will appeal to your friends. Mix personal favorites with one or two that you've never seen but have always been curious about. Pretty much everyone's seen *Pirates of the Caribbean*, *300*, and *The Lord of the Rings* a million times by now, so skip the most popular titles in favor of little-known gems that will open viewers' eyes to new cinematic worlds. Themes are fun. You can do a night of films about animals (*The Black Stallion, Duma, March of the Penguins*), animated classics (*Shrek, Yellow Submarine, Spirited Away*), or music films (*Walk the Line, La Bamba, Almost Famous*). If your fest will take place over the course of a single day, three films should be plenty. If you want to stretch it out for an entire weekend—as the main activity of a slumber party for three or four friends—choose five or six films (but don't feel pressured to watch them all if your audience is burning out). If your fest is a big hit, consider turning it into an annual event.

Not Your Mother's Munchies

Nowadays, lots of cinemas serve up a more diverse selection of high quality snacks to their customers. Follow their lead and, in addition to the customary popcorn, offer your friends (or ask them to bring) snacks like yogurt, granola, exotic juices, home-made cookies, and dark chocolate.

Mini Fest

Want to host a film fest, but don't have six hours? Pull together a mini fest with a handful of friends. Together, choose a theme—maybe comedy, sports, or romance, or a more specific one, like best slapstick or hardest breakup—and have each person pick a favorite scene from a movie based on that theme. Then have everyone cue up their tapes or DVDs at the right place, and play the scenes back to back at the mini fest. It's a great way to see parts of various movies all at once and to learn a little about some of your friends.

15 Throw a House Party

Parties are a big deal, and each one raises a ton of questions: Who's hosting? Who's on the guest list? Will the parents be out of town? Will the punch be spiked? Throwing a house party can be a blast, but it's important to make sure that your swanky get-together doesn't turn into an out-of-control mob scene. The last thing you want is a trashed living room, some jock puking on your mom's priceless Persian rug, and the cops showing up before midnight to close down the whole shebang. Careful planning will ensure that your shindig is remembered for all the right reasons.

How to Do It

First, make sure it's cool with your parents. Next, send out an invite. Try to limit your guest list to about 30 people since more will likely show up anyway. Invite all of your close friends and a few people you'd like to know better—having them over is a great way to move from the acquaintance phase to close-circle status. There's no need to go all out with a sit-down dinner, but do provide finger food and beverages. Music is a must, so create a playlist that works with the mood you want for the party—dance hall and hip-hop are sure to get rumps shaking, while downtempo house music will keep things more mellow and conversation-friendly.

Be Party Smart

To prevent your first house party from being your last, follow these guidelines:

1. Remove all breakables from arm's reach to ensure that even the most well-behaved guest doesn't accidentally knock over a crystal vase while dancing.

2. If alcohol somehow finds its way into your party, make sure to monitor it carefully; it *is* illegal, and if people drink too much, get crazy, or get hurt, you're screwed. (Plus, your parents may also get in trouble—not a great way to say "thanks" for the use of their space).

3. Do not post the invite online and ask your guests not to forward it to the entire school. If 75 people show up, shut it down—it's nearly impossible to weed out the crashers from the keepers in such a big group. The quickest way to empty a house? Tell 'em the cops are on their way.

4. Be sure to tell any immediate neighbors about your bash in advance, and ask them to call *you* (not the police) if things get too loud.

5. To help keep things relatively clean, have trash cans, dish towels, paper towels, TP, and carpet cleaner spray on hand at all times.

16 Read One Another's Palms

Life is so unpredictable. It's impossible to know what will happen tomorrow, let alone one, ten, or fifty years from now. Though your future depends primarily on your own life goals and your determination to reach them, it can be fun to experiment with different kinds of mysterious fortune-telling practices, like numerology, medicine cards, tarot cards, cootie catchers, the I Ching, and the Magic 8 Ball. And while most people have little faith in the pseudoscience of chiromancy—commonly known as palm reading—it can't hurt to try it, and it certainly makes for an entertaining afternoon with friends.

How to Do It

Gather with a few friends with open minds and open palms. Take turns studying the three most prominent lines on each other's palms. The heart line is found near the top of the palm. Its length and depth are thought to represent your love life, emotional stability, and blood-pumping health. The head line starts at the edge of the palm under the index finger, and supposedly indicates your intellectual and creative abilities. The life line runs from the edge of your palm above the thumb and forms an arc as it reaches your wrist. Believers will tell you that this line represents physical health and overall vitality and energy. Other lines that crisscross the three biggies include the sun line, fate line, and Girdle of Venus. To get diagrams, check out online illustrations, and, without taking it too seriously, see what the fates may (or may not) have in store for you.

Shake on It!

Once your palm-reading session has ended, keep your hands working by inventing a secret handshake to be used only by your close circle of friends. Whether it's a high-five adaptation or a spin-off of signals used in baseball practice, a secret handshake mystifies outsiders and ties friends together for life.

17 End an Argument

With all that's going on in your life, it's easy to find yourself every now and again in a tiff with a friend or relative. If you're already in a bad mood, you might mistake a friend's trying-to-be-helpful comment ("You've gotta work on your field goals if you wanna make varsity," or "Those pants make you look fat") as a vicious put-down. Miscommunications occur all the time. And backstabbing does happen, too, as groups of friends and foes form strategic alliances. Sometimes it's like high school is one long episode of *Survivor*. But real friends will weather the storm. So if you do offend your best friend or feel betrayed by a close pal's careless or callous comments, take the high road and bury the hatchet.

How to Do It

Once you've calmed down from the fight or slight, think objectively about the incident: Who said or did what, and why? Question the cause of the uproar, consider the motivations and feelings of everyone involved, and don't spare yourself when doling out blame or—just as important—forgiveness. Let's say a close friend mysteriously shunned you at lunch. Call, text, or email to find out what's really going on. Maybe he or she was just having a bad day. Hopefully a good heart-to-heart will clear up any misunderstanding. Were you out of line in insulting your friend's taste in music, or did you blow off plans because a better offer came along at the last minute? Own up to your mistake and vow to maintain mutual respect in the future. It'll feel good to clear the air and might just make you closer in the end.

When Judge Judy Is Busy

Need some help working out the argument or mending hurt feelings? Present both sides of the story to an unbiased third party—an older friend with great communication skills, or a trusted teacher or coach with a rep for always being fair—who can judge the situation and provide some much-needed perspective.

18 Correspond With a Pen Pal in Another Country

Your friends are probably a lot like you. They go to your school, or live on your block, or play on your team. Of course they're awesome, but there is also something to be gained from having a friend who lives halfway around the world. Corresponding with a pen pal from another country is a great way to learn about different cultures, practice your letter-writing skills, and develop the language you've been studying (or at least learn some key foreign phrases). Most important, you'll form a bond with a new friend, even if the two of you don't meet face-to-face for years.

How to Do It

Many schools have international exchange programs and keep lists of teens in other countries who want a pen pal from the states. Consult with them or check out an online site (*www.penpalworld.com* is a good one) that provides profiles of prospective pen pals so you can find someone—in India, Germany, Tahiti, or wherever—who shares some of your interests. Establish a steady back-and-forth correspondence and write at least once a month. Email is easy, but snail mail is actually more fun, as you have more time to anticipate the arrival of a letter from overseas (and can also start a collection of foreign stamps!). Be candid—you're writing to a trusted confidant who you don't actually have to see every day. Talk about hobbies, family, favorite books, and movies, and offer transatlantic tips on cool new bands. Make it a goal to cross paths eventually—a pen pal is a great excuse to take a cross-continental trip.

Can I Borrow 10 Bucks?

If your pen pal starts complaining about money problems, or goes so far as to ask you for a loan or gift, you might be dealing with a scam artist posing as a troubled teen. Stop the correspondence right away if anything seems suspicious.

19 Make a Gift

Exchanging thoughtful gifts with close mates on birthdays and winter holidays is a nice tradition and sincere gesture of appreciation. But if you really want to do something unique for your friends, give them handmade gifts. Your one-of-a-kind creations will make much more of an impression than the usual last-minute panic gift (DVD, cologne/perfume, video game). Making your own present also gives you a chance to be creative and saves you from handing over your last paycheck to some giant clothing or music corporation.

Time Is of the Essence

The reason people tend to buy instead of make gifts is because the latter takes *much* more time. If you've never made your gift idea before, factor in time to make mistakes and do-overs. Sure, Martha Stewart's three-minute segment on candlemaking looked realistic, but wax and wicks can turn on you, and a tricky task attempted last minute can leave you burned.

How to Do It

Take a look at your skills. Know how to make a mean death-by-chocolate brownie, toughen up a belt by adorning it with studs and grommets, or put together a slammin' mix of obscure ska jams? These are all perfect gift ideas. If you're taking an art, wordworking, or metalsmithing class on the weekends or as an elective in school, gift your original artwork adorned with your signature. Wordsmiths can write a short story or series of poems inspired by the recipient. If crafting is your thing, make a scarf, a pillow, or some homemade stationery in your buddy's fave color. If you're really stumped and can't come up with a homemade gift, make a donation to a worthy charity in your friend's name—it's socially responsible and très classy. A gift donation like this usually comes with a card or notice; put it in an envelope that you decorate and personalize for the recipient.

20 Start a Book Club

Losing yourself in a good book is one of life's most rewarding solitary pleasures. There's nothing quite so satisfying as whiling away a rainy Sunday afternoon with the latest David Sedaris stories or staying up way too late rereading a classic like *The Unbearable Lightness of Being* or *The Catcher in the Rye*. Reading can also be a great group activity. By forming a book club, you can share your love of literature with an intimate group of friends equally smitten with the written word. Remember: The point of a teen book club is not to create a setting of school-style drudgery, but rather to congregate with pals and have fascinating conversations about mysteries, romances, sci-fi weirdness, and other juicy topics not related to whatever whoever wore to school today.

How to Do It

Invite four to eight friends to join your book club. Members should commit to meeting once a month. Come up with a schedule of meeting dates and locations, and take turns playing host. Make a list of books you all want to read over the next year or so. If the group has a particular theme, make sure the joining members know that; if not, come up with a mix of novels, biographies, poetry collections, and other types of books that lend themselves well to analysis and debate. Include recent books, as well as older faves like *The Chronicles of Narnia*—it'll be interesting to hear others' impressions and interpretations of books you think you know inside out. At your meetings, discuss everyone's likes and dislikes about that month's book, and ask questions about plot points, themes, or characters that you didn't quite get. Don't be afraid to get personal—talk about how the story relates to your lives and dreams.

Suggested Reading

To start, here are seven can't-miss books for your club to read and discuss:

- *Girl With a Pearl Earring* by Tracy Chevalier

- *The Electric Kool-Aid Acid Test* by Tom Wolfe

- *The Secret Life of Bees* by Sue Monk Kidd

- *One Hundred Years of Solitude* by Gabriel García Marquez

- *White Oleander* by Janet Fitch

- *A Heartbreaking Work of Staggering Genius* by Dave Eggers

- *Life of Pi* by Yann Martel

21 Sing Karaoke

Trashing off-key *American Idol* contestants is a national pastime, but regardless of what Randy Jackson says, you've got to give even the most musically challenged Clay Aiken or Carrie Underwood wannabe credit for taking the stage in front of millions of viewers. Do you have the guts to share your rendition of "We Will Rock You" or "Somewhere Over the Rainbow" with snickering strangers? If you love to sing but aren't quite ready for the big leagues, gather a bunch of friends and grab a mic at a local karaoke club (or in the safety of your own home, where tone-deaf versions of classic ballads and trendy disco-diva hits are easily forgiven).

How to Do It

Most cities have at least one all-ages club where teens are welcome to channel their inner Mariah or Jay-Z on stage. Nothing happening in your town? Electronics stores sell home karaoke kits and preprogrammed microphones that are easy to use and feature hundreds of songs. Chip in with a few friends to buy one and have a karaoke party. Some cable providers also feature a karaoke channel, which runs the song lyrics across the screen. Whatever your karaoke scene and music source, the basics stay the same: Sing along to the recorded music, following the teleprompter if you need help with the lyrics. Don't hog the spotlight—and encourage shy friends to participate by choosing songs that are perfect for group sing-alongs, like "We Are Family" by Sister Sledge and "Bohemian Rhapsody" by Queen. Other surefire crowd-pleasers are "Baby Got Back" by Sir Mix-A-Lot, "Hey Ya!" by Outkast, "Somebody Told Me" by The Killers, and "I Will Survive" by Gloria Gaynor.

Who Invented Karaoke?

Karaoke, which means "empty orchestra" in Japanese, was invented by Japanese drummer Daisuke Inoue in Kobe in the 1970s. Inoue and his band often played gigs, which were attended by wealthy businessmen who liked to sing along. One time, a businessman asked the drummer to accompany him on a vacation to play music for him and his singing buddies. Inoue couldn't go, so he made the businessman a tape of his music to take with him. It was such a success that Inoue and his friends started making custom-made tapes for clients, and selling them together with singing machines. Thus, karaoke was born.

22 Dine High-End on a Low Budget

Fast food is cheap, and you don't have to worry about which fork to use when you're tearing into a burger or burrito at the mall's food court. But sometimes it's good to slow down and enjoy a different dining experience. Despite what you may think, fancy restaurants are not off-limits to you just because the special of the day is out of your price range. After all, it's the ambiance you're after, not the lobster. If you choose the place carefully, and order smartly, you can eat at a restaurant that uses real china and cloth napkins, and indulge in some serious epicurean splendor.

How to Do It

Scan reviews of nice new eateries in your paper's Food section or on any number of online restaurant guides. Pick your place according to the three As: atmosphere, accessibility, and … appetizers. This last one is important; order only starters, or what some restaurants refer to as "small plates" or "tapas," to keep your bill in check. (Be careful to order only one small dish per person, or you'll end up paying just as much as you would for entrées.) Opting for water instead of expensive drinks will save you tons—and it's amazing how much better water tastes when it comes in a fancy glass. Finally, even when you skimp a bit on dinner to save money, never do so with the tip. Restaurant staff work hard for their money and rely on tips for much of their income. Leave at least a 15 percent tip (which, to make the math easy, is about double the tax in lots of places). Raise that to 20 or 25 percent if your waitperson kicks butt.

A Sweet Way to Save

If you and your friends are really strapped but still want to hit up a fancy joint, skip dinner altogether and just go for dessert. If it is a busy restaurant, make sure to go a bit later in the evening after the dinner rush is over (restaurants don't like when people take up tables with small orders during dinnertime). Then, order some hot chocolate and cheesecake, and soak up the ambiance.

23 Take a Road Trip

Taking a road trip is a teenage rite of passage and a great opportunity to bond with buds while exploring new terrain. Even if you drive only a few towns over to enjoy a hike or visit friends who don't live nearby, you'll experience a newfound sense of freedom and responsibility. With the right group of friends, a well-stocked car, and a semi-set itinerary (leaving some room for spontaneous detours), you'll be ready to embark on an action-packed voyage of self-discovery.

How to Do It

Assemble a high-spirited crew, including at least a couple of people who have driver's licenses so no one is stuck behind the wheel for the entire trip. Your fellow road-trippers should be both responsible and easy going—you don't want to be piloted by a lunatic driver or have to deal with high-maintenance passengers who demand bathroom breaks every five miles. Jointly decide where you're headed. How about a local college where some friends go or a state park with hiking trails? Are you staying at a friend's place overnight or heading

Don't Forget

- maps
- food
- bottled water
- a change of clothes if needed
- CDs or an MP3 player for the car stereo
- a camera
- cell phones
- games, pillows, sleeping bags, or anything else needed to make the trip fun and comfy

back home the same day you leave? Make a solid plan and agree upon a basic budget before hitting the road. Everyone should chip in equally for gas, tolls, and other shared expenses, while food can be paid for individually. Don't forget to check out the car before you take off (apply the maintenance tips on page 178). And, before you get your kicks on Route 66, do make sure your parents know where you are going and what time you plan to be back. A charged cell phone will also ensure that they can get in touch with you, or vice versa, if need be.

Songs to Put on Your Road Trip Mix

"Born to Be Wild" — Steppenwolf

"Freebird" — Lynyrd Skynyrd

"Go West" — Liz Phair

"Driving" — PJ Harvey

"Gin and Juice" — Snoop Dogg

"The Rain (Supa Dupa Fly)" — Missy Elliot

"Wasn't Born to Follow" — The Byrds

"Me and Bobby McGee" — Janis Joplin

"Into the Great Wide Open" — Tom Petty & The Heartbreakers

24 Research Your Family Tree

You probably know where your parents were born—maybe you've even visited the cities or homes where they grew up. And if you're lucky enough to have grandparents in your life, you've hopefully heard some stories about their upbringings. But how about your great-grand-parents? Chances are they, or their parents, were not born in the United States. Know where they came from? Researching your family tree is a fascinating process. It'll put you in touch with your national and ethnic origins and make you see history not just as a dull subject to be studied in textbooks, but as something that you and your family are an integral part of. If you're adopted, you can do this for either your adopted or biological parents—both investigations will turn up interesting (and probably very different) results.

How to Do It

Tracing your ancestry is like putting together the pieces of a giant jigsaw puzzle—with each relative you locate, the whole family history becomes clearer. Start by talking to your parents and grandparents. Ask them to tell you everything they know about the family's genealogy. What countries did their ancestors emigrate from? Who first came to the US and when? Was the family name changed when the first arrivals docked on Ellis Island? Or when someone got married to someone else? Work with a hand-drawn chart, or download family tree worksheets from any number of websites (just type in "'family tree' and templates" into a search engine) dedicated to the pursuit.

Fill in blanks as you discover the names and origins of various relatives. Over the course of months or even years, you'll continue to make fascinating discoveries regarding the who, what, and where of your ancestors. Keep all information for posterity—future generations will thank you for doing the research.

Travel to the Source

Say you trace your family tree back through multiple generations, all the way to a small village in Chad, Portugal, Tasmania, Ukraine, or the Philippines. To get a sense of where you're originally from, travel to this place one day (barring any civil wars that might be occurring there) and check out your real hometown.

25 Reach Out to a Long-Lost Relative

While it's fun to use the Internet to piece together family history, there's plenty of investigating to do with those family members who are still alive. How many relatives do you actually communicate with on a regular basis? Even in big families, there are different inner circles that are knit pretty tightly. But somewhere out there you have relatives you've never even met, maybe never even knew you had. Maybe your grandfather has a younger sister he's no longer in touch with. Or what about the large, scattered family you have through a great-aunt's marriage to a diamond exporter who was born in New Zealand, raised in Tokyo, and retired in Delaware? Aren't you curious about these mysterious relatives you may look, sound, or act like? (If you're adopted and doing this with your unknown biological family, you're in for an even more challenging and fascinating journey.) By reaching out to a long-lost relative, you'll make genetic, geographical, and emotional connections, and learn more about yourself and your family.

How to Do It

Talk to your parents, cousins, aunts, and uncles, and see if they know about anyone floating around out there. Or pursue the family tree project on page 60 until you've turned up names and contact info that your parents and grandparents never had. You might hit some dead ends—old addresses or phone numbers, or maybe the relative in question has passed on. If all else fails, google them and see what comes up (make sure to put their first and last name in quotes when you search). Eventually, you're bound to locate a long-lost family member who will be thrilled to learn about you, too. If this person lives nearby, arrange for an in-person meeting. If states or countries separate you, start up email or snail mail correspondence.

Catch These Reunion Flicks

- *The Family Stone* (2005)—In this comedy, Dermot Mulroney takes Sarah Jessica Parker, his uptight girlfriend, home to meet his eccentric family.

- *Everything Is Illuminated* (2005)—Based on the novel by Jonathan Safran Foer, this comic drama stars Elijah Wood as a Jewish American who travels to Ukraine to find the woman who saved his grandfather during WWII.

- *The Royal Tenenbaums* (2001)—In this comedy with Gwyneth Paltrow, Ben Stiller, and the Wilson brothers, an estranged and wacky family full of former child prodigies reunites when the dad announces he is dying.

26 Record an Oral History

Uncle Joe is always good for an after-dinner walk down memory lane (especially if he's been sipping the cognac all evening). Why not get some of those great tales about the good ol' days on the record? Most people love to tell crazy stories about their childhoods, and most childhood stories, if you actually stop to listen, are pretty interesting. But a lot of this great info is gone or distorted after it's shared, unless someone has recorded it. The best way to preserve family stories and remember people's personalities is to do an oral history. By engaging a family member in tales of the past, you can learn a lot about history—from wars to economic depressions to pop culture, art, and dating rituals—and how it affected your family. And though hitting the Record button while Uncle Joe is mid-rant might be tempting, the idea here is to actually plan a proper session in which you interview a family member (or several) and record it on audio or video.

How to Do It

Approach a cool, older relative (like a grandparent or great-aunt or great-uncle) and let them know you'd like to do an oral history of them. Set up a time and a place and bring a list of questions to keep you on track, though you'll probably veer quite a bit from the list as you go. Depending on your resources and your subject's preference, you can record only audio (using a digital recorder or an old-school tape) or make a video (with a camcorder or digital camera)—just make sure that the material you record can be properly and safely stored for posterity on whatever medium you choose. Focus at first on biographical details such as date and place of birth, family names, marriage history, and home locations, but encourage your subject to go on tangents; as he or she talks about the past, all sorts of memories will come up. Make sure you get details—that's where the juicy stuff is. "So you said you were born *seven* months after your parents were married? And *why* was Aunt Betty nicknamed 'Hot Legs'?" Make sure your subject feels comfortable by offering to turn the recorder off at any point if they get nervous. As for yourself, pretend you're Oprah or Letterman interviewing a superstar ... who just happens to be one of your relatives.

Time It Right

Allot about two hours for each session. Any less and you won't get the nitty-gritty details. Any more and you'll wear out your subject with intense conversation. You can always resume with part deux on another day.

27 Spend Quality Time With Your Grandparents

For some teens, grandparents are fun, supportive elders who live nearby and take part in all major family activities. For others, Grandma and Grandpa are those kindly but somewhat distant folks who show up once or twice a year for dinner, bringing dicey-looking fruitcake and strange smells with them. Whether they're just around the corner, halfway across the country, totally hip or always complaining about their hip replacements, your grandparents should be an important part of your life. If any have passed on, be sure to keep their memories close by looking at photos, listening to recorded oral histories (if they exist), and talking to your remaining relatives about them. If they are alive and kicking, spend quality time with them while you still have the chance. You'll never regret it.

How to Do It

If any of your grandparents live nearby, set aside at least one afternoon or evening each month to spend with them. Plan appropriate activities depending on their health and mobility—dinner, good conversation, and a DVD at home (let them pick the film, or, if they are open-minded, introduce them to your faves) are simple ways to stay connected and share time. If they are active, spry, and up for an adventure, plan an overnight road trip or an outdoors activity like going to a fair or going sailing. When hanging out at home, ask them to show you photo albums, baby books, old letters, and keepsakes. Tell them about school, your friends, and your hobbies — and ask about their lives when they were your age. It's always interesting to compare generations. While on some levels your life is completely different from your grandparents' younger days, you may also find certain aspects of both surprisingly similar.

Grilling Gram and Gramps for Goods

Despite what you might think, your grandparents have a life beyond *Wheel of Fortune* and dinner at 4 pm. Ask them to teach you their secret talents. If your grandpa was once known for his four-alarm chili recipe, ask him to get in the kitchen and show you how it's done. Was your grandma an award-winning photographer back in the day? She could drop knowledge on how to frame subjects to make that perfect shot (even if she doesn't know the first thing about those "newfangled digital cameras").

28 Make Peace With a Sibling

Brothers and sisters are OK for the most part, but sometimes they can be a real pain in the *ss. Fights are an unavoidable part of growing up with siblings. Whether you're pummeling one another for some stupid reason, like not returning a borrowed book, or screaming about leaving the shared bathroom's toilet seat up or down, fights just plain suck. Feelings get hurt, objects get hurled across the room, and no one ever wins. Asking Mom or Dad to take sides isn't fair—they probably didn't even see what happened, and they're dealing with their own issues, anyway—so you've got to figure out a way to resolve these flare-ups yourselves. Next time you're embroiled in a nasty altercation with your bro or sis, vow to be the peacemaker. Even if you're sure you're right, swallow your pride for the sake of restoring some semblance of sanity to the household and be the one to end the battle.

How to Do It

As the situation heats up, try to maintain composure and remind yourself that two or more siblings living under one roof can't always avoid conflict. In fact, to some extent you probably thrive on it—you each want to assert independence and control (whether you realize it or not). Psychologists will tell you that older siblings think they know it all and hate being challenged by a younger family member, while younger siblings have not yet developed good reasoning skills and can be straight up immature. Although there may be some truth in these generalizations, refusing to play into these typical roles will curb the fight before it reaches the point of no return. If the scuffle escalates, point out the humor of the situation—come on, isn't arguing about last night's basketball game or who gets to control the remote pretty ridiculous? If you have no luck with the laugh tactic, or the argument is about something more serious, retreat to opposite ends of the house and take time to cool down. Then try to talk things out more calmly. The key is to learn how to communicate better so that when you do have disagreements you'll be able to hash them out

minus any brawling. With heightened communication skills and a little luck, you'll be able to peacefully share the house—for a little while longer, anyway.

The Parent Trap

If you and your siblings fight incessantly, shift the emphasis away from your differences and instead focus on what you have in common—namely, how much your parents drive you crazy. It'll make you remember that though you two have some significant issues, you're actually comrades on the same team.

29 Plan a (Cool) Family Outing

O h, the dreaded forced family outing. We've all had to endure trips to yet another staging of the *Nutcracker* (I got dressed up for this?), painfully boring family reunions (Will Aunt Shenee ever lay off the "when I was your age" stories?), or treacherous camping weekends (if I kill my brother inside the tent, does it still count as manslaughter?). But if your parents and/or stepparents are the "quality time" type, family outings can be tough to avoid. Certainly there must be a happy medium in which you can kick it without wanting to kill one another. Try to crack the code and take matters into your own hands by planning an outing that might actually be … fun.

One-on-Ones

If you actually *like* your family, then spending time with the gang is a real treat. But it's equally vital that you get in some one-on-one time with each parent. Be sure to spend quality time alone with just Mom or Dad at least once a month. (If your parents are split up, you may be doing this quite a bit already without even realizing it.)

How to Do It

First, strike a deal with your 'rents—tell them that if they pony up the cash, you'll plan the outing. (They might not trust you at first, so be prepared to present some trip details before receiving any personal checks or credit card numbers.) Now, decide where to go. Why not buck convention and plan an activity your family rarely does together? (No, "getting along" doesn't count.) If you're usually cooped up in the multiplex, plan an outdoorsy activity like picking apples at an orchard, cycling around town on tandem bikes, or riding the rapids on a rafting expedition. Want to get out of the sun or snow for a change? Scan the newspaper for an interesting museum exhibition, or hit up a pool hall. And if you know that you can't make it through one day without wanting to beat your brother silly, plan a little friendly competition during lunchtime. A picnic-style poker game or vicious Scrabble showdown will allow you and your siblings to have it out under the guise of sweet family togetherness.

30 Cook a Three-Course Dinner

"What's for dinner?" If you're usually asking this question, try answering it one night (undoubtedly to the shock and delight of your household's resident chef). Cooking a three-course dinner might seem daunting if your previous preparations have been limited to late-night Hot Pockets, but the process can be simple and fun. Think of the kitchen as equal parts art studio and scientist's lab, where you can express your epicurean desires and concoct creative dishes that can't be found on the menu at Mickey D's or T.G.I. Friday's. If that's not motivation enough, consider this: The stomach is the way to the heart. Learn how to cook and you'll score big with future college crushes.

How to Do It

For meal ideas, specific ingredients, and instructions, look through cookbooks at home—they're probably stashed away on a kitchen shelf—or surf the web for the thousands of helpful sites featuring recipes both simple and advanced. Determine the number of people you're cooking for and purchase the right amount of ingredients based on your recipe instructions. When in doubt, buy extra; it's always better to have leftovers than to tell Dad or your big sis that they'll have to settle for PB&J sandwiches. Keep in mind your family members' particular food faves and dietary restrictions, and adapt your three-course meal to suit their tastes, using unusual seasonings (harissa, curry, and saffron) and dressings (tahini or flax oil with vinegar) to spice up popular standbys such as grilled chicken and chef salads. Presentation counts, too, so throw on some cool garnishes (sprig of rosemary for a meat dish or asturshins atop a frisée salad), and opt for nice dishes as opposed to the plastic three-compartment plates tucked away with the wooden chopsticks in the kitchen's scary random-things drawer. And don't forget, as the cook, you're exempt from clean up duty.

Classic Salmon Dinner

Start with a healthy salad of mixed greens and lots of fresh veggies, move on to broiled salmon (toss a few lemon slices on top and put in the broiler for 10 minutes), and send 'em to bed full and happy with your signature peach cobbler for dessert. Bon appétit!

31 Prepare a Presentation for a Special Event

S ure, you've had to make countless presentations for classes over the years—teachers have demanded speeches on plate tectonics, the division of cells, and just about every other blah topic out there. But how often have you taken those skills out of the classroom and voluntarily made a presentation for someone you actually like? Next time you attend a friend or family member's special day—be it a birthday, Bar or Bat Mitzvah, confirmation, or graduation—surprise them with a presentation that pays homage to their general fabulousness. It's an unexpected gift that will not only impress the ones you love, but also be remembered far better than another kitchy knick-knack that's destined for the junk drawer.

How to Do It

Whether you're celebrating privately as a family or at a huge party with tons of friends and relatives, prepare a presentation that suits the honoree. Say your older brother is graduating from college—make a speech in which you highlight all the ways he's inspired you (including the tips he gave you on how to sleep your way through class on the sly). Save your sister's Sweet 16 from becoming a pop music nightmare by playing an original or classic song for her on your instrument of choice. For your parents' anniversary, edit home movies together and screen the family epic at their celebration. For an engagement party, you can take a cue from Dr. Seuss and compose a rhyming poem chock-full of little jokes. Your best friend's graduation party? Compile a slide show of the honoree set to music and include the "can't believe we did that" pic of your shared faux modeling session back in second grade and that shot proving that a bowl cut is *always* a bad idea.

Record for Posterity

Document your presentation—10 years from now, at another special family to-do, you can play the video of you making the speech or singing the self-composed "Grandma Song" that everyone in attendance still talks about. Your family will love it, and you'll get a good laugh out of it, too.

32 Learn a Martial Art

Some people become interested in martial arts because they want to be able to kick butt, but learning to punch and block with graceful precision is only one by-product of studying a martial art. Many exercise gurus actually insist that the best all-around workout is martial arts, and practicing tai chi, karate, kung fu, or one of the other ancient Asian traditions will sharpen your mind as much as it tones your body. Plus, as you gain an understanding of the philosophies behind your practice, you'll learn about the importance of calm, restraint, and balance in life—not lessons to be taken lightly. Oh, and with most disciplines, you'll learn to kick butt, too.

How to Do It

Many gyms and martial arts studios offer classes for teenagers at all levels. Observe some classes or attend a tournament to learn about the different disciplines. Tae kwon do emphasizes foot and fist maneuvers, while jujitsu involves lots of grappling and throwing, and hapkido focuses on channeling energy through circular motions and carefully coordinated punches. Many martial arts have a strong spiritual base. There are dozens of types, each one with its own traditions. Make sure you find an experienced instructor who has studied for several years (or even decades) and has a solid knowledge of the physical and philosophical aspects of the practice. As you progress in your study, you'll be given a special rank or a series of colored belts that indicate your skill level. Stick with it and you may establish a lifelong relationship with martial arts, and potentially with your teacher, too.

Enter the Dragon

World-famous martial arts master Bruce Lee popularized high-energy self-defense on the big screen in the 1970s, starring in *Fist of Fury* and other box office hits. Even though Bruce died at the mere age of 32, he paved the way for other onscreen martial artists like Jackie Chan and Jet Li. Check out one of his classics on DVD.

33 Establish an Exercise Routine

Sitting on the sofa all afternoon, watching *South Park* or *Sex in the City* reruns and eating Häagen-Dazs straight from the container may be fun once in a while, but it shouldn't be your daily MO. It's important to get physical on a regular basis, or you'll wind up cheating your bod of feel-good endorphin releases that elevate your mood and self-image. You don't have to be a sports nut to enjoy the benefits of exercise. You can find tolerable (enjoyable, even) ways to get your sweat on. It's much better to get into the habit of working out now, when you're still bursting with energy, rather than waiting until you're older and in dire need of shedding extra pounds in order to avoid getting a heart attack from your next bag o' chips. Whether you like lifting weights at the gym, jogging through the park, taking a kickboxing class, or doing crunches in the privacy of your own bedroom, establishing and sticking to an exercise routine will strengthen your body, mind, and spirit—and get you more attention in the hallway.

How to Do It

Start by finding out your heart rate, body weight, waist and muscle measurements, and body fat percentage. Gym memberships usually include a free consultation with a trainer who will administer these tests and record the results so you can track your progress over the coming months (don't worry, they keep these stats confidential). Determine your goals—do you want to tone your tummy, get energized, gain muscle strength, or pump up your pecs? Talk with a trainer to decide on a workout routine that meets your goals. Be sure to be honest with them. If they envision a two-hour a day regimen and you know that ain't gonna happen, let them know so they can design a workout that will better fit your needs. If you're not into the gym scene, you can exercise at home or get a great cardio workout by riding your bike to and from school. (Just towel off before heading into homeroom.) Jazz up your workout routine by trying new activities such as yoga, rock climbing, swimming, or tennis—it may turn into a life-long love.

Stay Motivated

It's easy to fall out of a workout routine. You miss a day because of a test or a cold and before you know it, six months have gone by and you haven't lifted anything but your head off the couch. To stay motivated, hook up with a friend who will keep you committed and give you the proper flack (aka guilt) if you start engineering lame excuses for missing your afternoon run. And keep an exercise log or journal that tracks your progress over the months (muscle gained, weight lost, miles run per day); seeing the changes on paper will inspire you to stick with it.

34 Enter a Sports Competition

Between schoolwork, our relationships with our friends and families, and making life decisions, we challenge ourselves all the time. But how often do we challenge our bodies? It's good to put your physical self to the test, and entering a sporting competition is a great way to push your endurance without committing to a season of practices and games. Enter a mini marathon like a 2K—or 5K, if you're bold. Join a weekend-long volleyball tournament organized by your parks and rec department, or participate in a ski challenge set up by your hometown resort. When running, spiking, or skiing alongside other contestants, your otherwise dormant competitive spirit will emerge—and you'll find yourself pushing extra hard to try to come out on top. The adrenaline rush is an incredible feeling (whether you win or not).

Find the Right Fuel

There's nothing worse than training for weeks, only to feel funny the day of the event. What we eat has a huge effect on how we perform, so it's smart to fuel your body with the right stuff before your competition. Some people have a carb-heavy meal the night before a big race or load up on water in the few days before a mogul challenge. Check with an authority on your sport for tips on how to fuel your body, avoid stomach cramps, and be at your best.

How to Do It

Search the Internet for upcoming events in your area (companies like Nike sponsor runs in cities across the country), or contact your city's parks and rec department for other organized competitions. You're likely to find a ton of options, but be judicious with your choice—while it's fun to try something new, it's wise to avoid ultimate Frisbee if you don't like objects flying at your face. Once you find a challenge you're up for, it's time to train. Professional marathoners prepare for months before the actual race. Even if you're not running 26 miles or playing a sport for an entire season, you still have to prep your body. If you don't know what you should be doing to get ready, other than practicing the sport itself, ask the event organizer for advice—it may turn out that Pilates is the secret training tip for volleyballers who continuously slam the ball with that super-extended reach.

35 | Determine Your Blood Type

Y ou might recall covering blood type in some distant biology class—or you might not. Unlike memorizing the kingdom and phylum of every species, knowing your blood type is vital. The red stuff comes in many varieties, and it's important to know what yours is in case you ever need to give blood or receive a transfusion. Blood types have to be compatible in order for a transfusion to be safe. The four main groups are: A, B, AB, and O. Here's a quick rundown.

- O is the universal donor; if you are an O, you can give to anyone, but only receive blood from other Os.

- AB is the universal recipient; if you are an AB, you can get blood from anyone, but only give to someone else who is AB.

- A and B types can give to their types (A or B) and to ABs, and receive from their types (A or B) and Os.

The antigens on the surface of your red blood cells determine your blood type and each type can be either positive or negative. No type is better or worse than another—it's all just ... blood.

How to Do It

A great way to find out your blood type is to participate in a blood drive. Many schools hold them, and all you need to do is get a release form signed by a parent. (There are age restrictions, and certain people can't donate blood for health reasons, so get the details from the folks running the drive.) If you donate blood, you'll soon receive a postcard or letter in the mail that tells you what your blood type is. You can also ask your doctor the next time you go in for a checkup; if he or she doesn't have it on record, request that your blood is typed the next time you need to have blood taken for a routine exam. Regardless of how you find out your blood type, write it down and then learn the types of your immediate family members. It's good to know, in case of emergency.

She's Just Not My Type

In South Korea and Japan, blood type is common knowledge and frequently discussed among friends. It's sort of like comparing astrological signs.

36 Study Food Labels

Y ou are what you eat, right? So do you really want to identify yourself as a gelatinous mass of high fructose syrup, partially hydrogenated vegetable oil, and monosodium glutamate? By reading the labels on canned and packaged food before digging in, you'll learn a whole lot about the nutritional value—or lack thereof—of your favorite meals and snacks. Labels not only give us a complete list of ingredients, but they also tell us how much (or how little) nutritional value our food contains in terms of things like protein, carbs, fat, and vitamins.

How to Do It

The US Food and Drug Administration requires that every food can and package comes with a "Nutrition Facts" label. The first thing the label lists is the number of servings per container. Typical serving sizes are one cup of cereal, five pretzels, and two cookies. But get real—who eats only two cookies? Scan the label for info on the amount of calories, types of fat (trans fats typically yield no nutritional benefits, while unsaturated fats, like those found in avocados, do a body good), cholesterol, sugar, sodium, carbohydrates, and protein per serving. Amounts are given as a percentage of the total daily recommended intake, based on a 2,000-calorie-per-day diet (which is intended for an averaged-size person, so if you are bigger or smaller, adjust accordingly). Calories indicate the amount of energy you'll get from eating a typical portion. Calories also contribute to weight gain, so try not to pig out on high-calorie foods. On the label, you'll also see percentages of different vitamins and minerals, such as calcium and iron. These nutrients are measured in grams (represented by a "g") or milligrams ("mg"). If it's all a bunch of zeroes in this section, you're not getting many nutrients out of your chow. When reading the ingredients, look for simple words you recognize, like eggs, coconut, almonds, and olive oil. Steer clear of food that contains a lot of things you can't pronounce. Those ingredients are generally food additives and are composed of high dosages of artificial salt and sugar. They wreak havoc on your immune system and should be nixed in favor of things with fewer syllables.

Additives to Avoid

Be on the lookout for these unhealthy artificial additives:

- Yellow 5 (aka tartrazine)
- Sodium chloride
- Olestra
- Sodium nitrate
- Yeast extract
- … and all food color dyes

O K … before you start thinking, "Detox? That's for druggies," consider this: Most of us are total food junkies. Whether we are candy fiends, pizzaholics, or burger bingers, we all have addictions of some kind. Do you eat calorie-rich triple cream cheese? Devour cans of sugar-loaded soda? Sure, food is a perfectly legal vice—but it is still a vice and can get out of control. Practice the ultimate form of self-discipline and detoxify your system. There are a few ways to do it. You can remove toxins from your diet, add something (like leafy greens) to the mix, or choose a combination of the two. If your daily breakfast consists of Skittles and Mountain Dew and you tend to down sugar throughout the day, try going sugar-free for a week. If you've been overeating lately (which happens a lot during the holiday season), try to fast for a day, drinking only nutritious juices and water. Giving your bogged-down system a fresh start will not only cleanse your conscience of your less-than-stellar dietary behavior, but it will also make your system run smoother—and that's a difference you'll feel.

How to Do It

First, identify what your "drug" is; sugary drinks, candy, and fries are common culprits. Next, decide how you're going to reign yourself in. Like with nicotine, quitting sugar cold turkey can spawn a short temper and irritability—so you may decide to cut back on your intake for a few days (by drinking just two sodas a day, for example) before going all the way. If you're detoxing from red meat, be sure to load up on other types of protein such as beans, fish, or soy products to keep your energy levels up. After you've established a detox plan, set goals (three days without cookies!) and reward yourself (with a trip to the movies or spa treatment … not a cookie). Finally, be sure to pay attention to how your body reacts to your detox. You may feel less lethargic (in which case, you might want to consider detoxing for good), or you might feel weak (in which case, you might need a little of the very thing you were cutting out). Most important, listen to your body and be sure to adjust your detox plan in accordance with any health issues, allergies, or sensitivities; while any form of detox may feel like torture at first, the point is to rejuvenate your system, not harm it.

Fast Facts

Fasting can be a great way of purifying the system, but it has to be done very carefully. Our bodies require nutrients and lots of hydration. While skipping heavy meals for a day isn't likely to hurt us, it's best to read up on fasting techniques or talk to a doctor or nutritionist about the method that's right for you. And fasting is NOT a way to lose weight. So don't use it as an excuse for dangerous, excessive dieting. Depriving your body of food for days on end will leave you with vitamin deficiencies, metabolic issues, and a whole host of problems you didn't bargain for.

38 Plant an Herb Garden

In ancient times, Greeks and Romans used herbs to purify banquet halls. Greeks associated thyme with courage and sacrifice, while Romans believed it was a cure for coughs and hangovers. Romans also adorned Olympic champions with bay leaves. In the middle ages, rosemary was administered as a tranquilizer and cure-all. Today, herbs like caraway, oregano, and tarragon are commonly used as ingredients in salads, seafood, and meat dishes. Chinese medicine is based on the idea that herbs can treat just about any ailment. If you've never stopped to think about the herbs you eat, now is a good time. From sage to cilantro to dill, they add scent and flavor to all sorts of food and are surprisingly useful on their own. Planting an indoor herb garden is simple and rewarding. With the right light, enough water, and some green-thumbed TLC, you can nurture herbs from seed to sprout in just a few weeks.

How to Do It

With proper treatment, herbs will grow indoors all year. Shop around for several smallish planters (3- or 4-inch pots placed in a tray that will hold water) and the right kind of soil mix (ask the salesperson at the store). Choose a selection of seeds—some herbs will thrive and others won't, so experiment with different types. Plant a few seeds in each pot, leaving an inch of gravel at the bottom so that excess water will drain. Place the pots near a window that gets sunlight from the south or west. Keep the soil moist, but don't over-water—once or twice a week should do it. Within a couple of weeks you'll start to see little baby herbs poking out of the soil. Snip off a few leaves, run them under cold water, pat them dry, and add them to your meals. If plants, such as basil, start to flower, pinch the flower off to keep the plant growing more leaves.

A Medley of Scents and Flavors

Try growing and cooking with these lesser-known herbs:

- **anise:** tangy in salads as an herb and sweet in cookies in seed form

- **borage:** tastes a bit like cucumber and is delicious in iced tea and lemonade

- **chervil:** tastes similar to parsley and perfect for most soups and cheese soufflés

- **hyssop:** has a pungent taste and can be mixed into onion dip

- **lovage:** tastes similar to celery and yummy in soups and salads

39 Know Your Silhouette and Colors

Thanks to hyperstyled music videos, hip-hop moguls starting their own lines, and celebs plugging just about every brand out there, fashion pervades our lives. Are plaids totally retro? Can I wear white after Labor Day? Is orange the new black? It can be hard to keep up with trends, but fashion is about more than that. It's about having a personal style that expresses who you are at this moment in your life. By paying just a little attention to your body type and the clothes and colors that flatter your frame and skin tone, you can develop a unique style that's based on individuality and feeling attractive, and not about what *GQ* or *Vogue* dictates.

How to Do It

Figuring out your body type, or silhouette, helps determine what sorts of clothes look best on you. Most guys are built like a solid rectangle, while girls can have rectangle, triangle, inverted triangle, or hourglass shapes. To determine your silhouette, go online and search for "body shape" and "style." If you look at various sites, you'll find silhouette illustrations, clothing recommendations, and makeover tips.

As for what color clothing looks best on you, fashion experts look at your skin, eyes, and hair for complementary tones. One approach is to go straight to the mall and ask a professional to assess what colors are best for you. Some department stores employ image consultants who love to talk all day about this stuff (think Carson from *Queer Eye for the Straight Guy*), and many cosmetic counters do the same. Hitting them up for tips won't cost you a penny—unless you somehow get sucked into buying a boatload of cosmetics.

What Season Are You?

In the world of fashion, you'll sometimes hear people talk about what season they are; it's a concept that beauty professionals use to figure out what colors look best on people. Check out the graph below and see where you fall. Fit into more than one category? You are probably a mix of seasons—most people are.

	skin undertones	hair color	eye color	the colors that look good on you
Winter	blue or pink undertones	brunettes	dark eyes	white, black, navy blue, red, shocking pink
Summer	blue or pink undertones	natural blondes and brunettes	pale eyes	pastels, lavender, plum, rose-brown, soft blue
Autumn	golden undertones	redheads and brunettes	golden brown eyes	beige, orange, gold, dark brown
Spring	golden undertones, freckles	straw-colored or strawberry-blonde hair	blue/green eyes	peach, golden yellow, golden brown

40 Learn About Safe Sex

OK, you know the drill: If you're going to be intimate with a guy or a girl during your teenage years (or ever), you have to be safe about it. You've grown up in the era of safe sex education, and even if your parents or community leaders have tried to shelter you from reality, you know full well from friends, teachers, and maybe even your own experiences that the big league pleasures of physical love and hormonal lust come with some big league risks (like STDs and unwanted pregnancies). Sex doesn't have to be a scary topic. Ask a lot of questions, educate yourself, and keep your body safe. And that also means saying "no" to sex if you're not ready—which is a perfectly adult move that, unlike saying "yes" when you're unsure, is never followed by regret.

No Means No

Never let anyone pressure you into having sex, whether it's your first time or your fifth. This goes for girls as well as boys. To have or not have sex is a totally personal choice, and only you can decide when and with whom you want to share the experience.

How to Do It

Sure, it's difficult and a little embarrassing to talk about sex with your parents, but in most cases they will appreciate your willingness to be open and honest about such an important topic. If you just don't have that type of relationship with Mom and Dad, talk to your doctor, a health counselor at school, or another knowledgeable adult about safe sex. Planned Parenthood is an excellent and affordable resource for basic information and counseling. Are you aware of various methods of birth control? Do you know how to properly use a condom? There's no room for error with this stuff, so ask the experts before bumbling through an awkward or unsafe experience with a partner.

41 Get a Passport

Traveling outside your own country for the first time is one of the most exciting things you'll do, but it also requires careful planning. A solid backpack and a well-thought-out itinerary help a lot, but they won't do you any good without a passport. In fact, due to a law passed in the beginning of 2007, you even need a passport to fly to our bordering countries, Mexico and Canada. A passport is your ticket to crossing national borders and embarking on jet-setting adventures. The little blue booklet contains your name, place and date of birth, specially assigned identification number, and headshot (photo of your face), and is checked by airport and border officials anytime you leave the US and enter or exit any other country. The point of having a passport is to prove that you are who you say you are, and not some wackjob traveling with a fake ID. Even if you're not planning on an international trip just yet, it's still good to get a passport; processing can take a long time, so getting it sorted out now means you won't have to rush if a travel op suddenly comes your way.

How to Do It

Check out the government travel site, *www.travel.state.gov*, for the nearest passport office location, and download and fill out the application form before you go to save time. Be prepared to wait: Lines can be unbelievably long. You need to bring your own passport photos, which are small official pictures that you can have taken at designated places, like certain photo booths, drugstores,

and travel agencies. They show your full face, with open eyes, from the tip of your head to the top of your shoulders. (Warning: Like most official pictures, passport photos tend to make you look a little less gorgeous than you really are.) Along with your photos, you must bring proof of identification and US citizenship. A certified birth certificate and driver's license or other government-issued ID card work best, but if you don't have these, see the government site for other options. If you're under 18, your parent or guardian will need to be present and provide consent. Processing fees are close to $100. Your passport should take about six weeks to arrive. When you get it, be sure to put it in a safe place—it's a total pain to replace.

42 Visit a Foreign Country

While journeying to another country is pretty ambitious, and certainly not something all teens have the opportunity to do, you should jump at the chance if it comes along. Visiting a foreign country opens your eyes to other people, customs, and ways of life fascinatingly different from your own. Despite Disney's lyrical promise, it's not really a small world after all, but rather a ginormous, endlessly complex global network of far-flung locales from Argentina to Zimbabwe. Even Canada, though similar in culture and relatively nearby, makes for an exciting trip. There's much more to planet Earth than your own backyard—and, souvenirs are way cooler when you've had to haggle over prices in another language.

How to Do It

A Mexican cruise with 10 pals is a pipe dream for most, especially in terms of getting the parental OK, so you'll need to get more creative with your adventure planning. One option is to bark up the family tree and seek out any relatives living in other countries. How could your dad deny you the chance to bond with a long-lost uncle, or the opportunity to get a sense of your roots beyond the Red, White, and Blue? If your family strictly resides in the US of A, investigate an international exchange program (like American Field Service—*www.afs.org*) in which you live with a family in another country while in school or during the summer. When presenting the details to your parents, tell them as much as possible about the organization you'd like to go with, the host country you want to visit, the fees involved, and scholarships offered. If you play your cards right, you'll soon be practicing a foreign language firsthand and meeting cute new potential dates— with accents.

Another State of Mind

If you want to travel but can't venture out of the country just yet, venture into another US state. Midwest residents should check out a coastal locale (California and New York are worlds unto themselves), beach bums should surf inland turf (deep in the heart of Texas), and everyone should consider a visit to national treasures such as Monument Valley in Utah and Arizona and Mount Rushmore in South Dakota. Teen tours go to lots of these places and not all of them will break the bank.

43 Learn a Foreign Language

I f you're using the time spent in Spanish class to catch up on zzzs, you might want to reconsider where you take your siestas. Learning a foreign language is totally worth the time and effort and you'll be glad you stuck with it once you're past the "Hola. ¿Què tal?" phase. Nearly one in five US residents over the age of 4 speaks a language other than English at home, and knowing another language makes foreign travel so much easier. Sure, reading Hebrew (right to left), writing in Tagalog, or speaking Maltese is challenging at first, but becoming bi- or even trilingual will make you worldly and sophisticated, even if it's some time until you leave your hometown.

Don't Wait

Most people decide they want to learn a foreign language later on—like when they are in their twenties—but it's best not to wait. Once you leave high school, lessons get pretty pricey. It's also way easier to pick up a language at 16 than 26 or 36.

How to Do It

Stop taking power naps during language class at school. Better yet, make language study an extracurricular activity so it feels more like fun and less like homework. Shop around for CDs and MP3s featuring easy-to-follow grammar and conversation lessons. Listen to them on headphones for total immersion, and don't be shy about repeating phrases aloud as you hear them for the hundredth time—repetition is the key to language mastery. You can also listen to music in foreign languages, which is a great way to increase your vocab. Get together once a week with friends who are similarly eager to pick up German or Mandarin, and, if you know any native speakers, hang out with those who are willing to point out your mistakes—and teach you curse words. You can also swap lessons with another person who already speaks the language you're studying. Stick with it and, before you know it, you'll be a polyglot.

"oye como va"

Whether you realize it or not, you regularly take part in various cultural traditions, both on special occasions and in your daily life. Some of those traditions may be handed down from relatives who were born in other countries; others are American traditions that are so ingrained you likely don't see them as traditions at all (like doing the wave at a baseball game or setting off fireworks on July 4). But do you ever take time to purposefully learn a new tradition from someone else's culture? With so many ethnicities represented in the US, you can explore foreign cultures without going very far. Everywhere you look, there are tons of traditions, parties, rituals, and holidays to take part in, from Japanese tea ceremonies and Tunisian henna art to Scottish kilt-wearing and Mexican Dia de los Muertos fiestas.

How to Do It

Ask friends from various cultural backgrounds how they celebrate their homelands and histories, or what unusual daily customs their families practice. Then join them in observing these customs and their special holiday traditions. Jewish friends might invite you into their *sukkah*—which is a temporary, hand-built house—to eat a tasty dinner during Sukkot, a yearly harvest festival. Argentines like to share a cup of maté, an antioxidant-rich green tea drink that everyone sips from the same *bombilla*, or straw. Thai friends might show you a new recipe, and Korean friends may teach you to remove your shoes before entering the house. Another way to become more worldly is to go to community centers, which host lots of cultural events. And many restaurants feature special menus commemorating ethnic holidays, so you can pig out on something other than burgers for a change.

All for One, One for All

Some traditions unite all cultures, such as the International Day for Tolerance. Everyone is encouraged to celebrate this universal plea for nonviolence on November 16. For info on this and other occasions inclusive of all cultures, visit *www.betterworldcalendar.com.*

45 Visit Your State Capital

You probably memorized all 50 state capitals back in grade school, but have you ever visited the political center of your own state, let alone any capitals of the other 49? They're not always the most glamorous cities (Sacramento instead of San Francisco? Albany instead of NYC?), but they do house our country's leaders in architecturally diverse buildings that boast golden domes and decent gift shops. Boise and Baton Rouge, Concord and Carson City, Topeka and Tallahassee—tour the capital closest to home, then fan out. Bonus points if you ever get to Juneau and Honolulu.

How to Do It

Many schools sponsor trips to the capital, but you can also take it upon yourself to head to Montgomery, Dover, Cheyenne, or wherever with your family or some friends. Pile in the car and drive the dozens or hundreds of miles (longer distances deserve a cheesy motel stopover) to that locus of political intrigue, historical happenstance, and tourist-trap gift shops. Call or email in advance to see if it's necessary to arrange a tour of the capitol buildings, and ask if you can shake hands with a legislator while you're there. Get a map with the main attractions, then mosey around to learn about your state's history, most likely rooted in false promises and bloodshed—but fascinating nonetheless.

Chillin' With George and Abe

The capital of capitals is, of course, Washington, DC. Buzzing with political scandal and studded with monuments to great (and not so great) presidents, the District of Columbia is pretty awesome no matter what time of year you visit, from the snowy winter to the humid summer to the milder seasons in between. More than a dozen world-class museums are all free of charge. For everything you need to know, check out *www.dc.gov*.

46 Take a Camping Trip

Mix trekking through fields of wildflowers, bathing in an aqua-marine pond, and sleeping under the stars with getting attacked by bloodthirsty mosquitoes, being forced to use leaves for toilet paper, and eating cold beans straight from the can, and you get the amazing and equally challenging experience of camping. Even though leaving behind creature comforts can take some getting used to, it's a small price to pay to commune with nature. Whether with relatives, friends, or a community group, camping for a few days will instill deep appreciation for natural splendor, survival skills, and your comfy bed back home.

How to Do It

Here are some tips to planning a successful camping trip.

- Gather a group of people that includes at least one or two who have camped before.

- Decide if you want to do car camping, stay in a cabin, or go for the full-on tent experience, then thoroughly research the best spot for your outdoors excursion. Kampgrounds of America (*www.koa.com*) is a great resource for finding nice, clean campsites that have good facilities.

- Check that the weather is reasonable where you are going; there can be huge climate changes only miles from home, and camping in cold weather is not for the faint of heart.

- Bring a warm sleeping bag, plenty of food and water, insect repellent, some music (or, even better, instruments to play), flashlights with extra batteries, good hiking shoes (waterproof!), rain gear, sunscreen, and a journal and camera to record your adventures.

- When pitching your tent, remember that spots farther from the water are usually less buggy and locations surrounded by trees will protect you from wind and sun.

- Pitch your tent on dry, flat ground void of big rocks and anthills. (If your tent is on slanted ground, position your head uphill.)

If you don't have wheels to travel or can't get permission from your parents to spend a night out in the woods, consider what lies beyond your back door. Pitching a tent in the backyard is a great warm-up for bigger adventures … and you won't have to go far if you have to hit the commode in the middle of the night.

Bring It In, Pack It Out

When camping, be sure to take out everything you brought in with you, including any granola bar wrappers, empty water bottles, and other non-biodegradable items. When going number 2 in the woods, dig a 6-inch hole, do your business, and cover the hole. You can also bury used TP, or put it all into a secured plastic bag that you can dispose of in a trash can when you're back in civilization.

47 Hike to a Mountaintop

I f you're feeling stuck about a decision, or just in life in general, it's important to bust out of your day-to-day and get a new perspective on things. One of the best ways to do this is to climb a high peak and gaze down at the world below. Hiking to a mountaintop is not only excellent exercise in the great outdoors but also a trip from the known to the unknown, an adventure in which the journey is just as important as the destination. You don't have to conquer Mount Everest or scale Kilimanjaro (yet). In fact, the point is not to *conquer* a mountain, period—it's to become a part of it. So start by setting your sights on an accessible summit and plan to spend a day (or two) absorbed in the grandeur of Mama Nature.

How to Do It

Hikes are more fun, and much safer, when you go with friends or relatives, so recruit a companion or two to join you. With your hiking partner(s), study a local map and pinpoint the mountain you want to climb. It should be a well-traveled mountain (especially if you're not an experienced trekker) with a clearly marked path. You can get more information about local hikes from your state's parks and rec department or a website like *www.localhikes.com*.

To prepare, make sure you pack the following.

- **plenty of water:** It's easy to get dehydrated at high altitudes, especially if the weather isn't hot enough to remind you to drink. Drink a bit of water before beginning the climb and sip along the way.

- **sandwiches and snacks:** You'll work up quite an appetite after a mile or two of uphill trekking.

- **sunscreen:** Even if the weather is mild, pull a mom move and protect your skin—getting burned is a total drag and happens even in cloudy conditions.

- **a hat or sunglasses:** This will keep the sun out of your eyes.

- **a camera:** Have one handy for those great photo ops, which are also good excuses to take breathers.

Once you reach the top, reward yourself with a nice rest and some quiet moments of contemplation before you head back down to the world below.

Flora and Fauna

Learn how to recognize poison ivy, poison oak, and other problematic plants, and find out if any wildlife is known to roam the terrain. Snakes might be cool in cages, but when out in the wild they can get a little ... territorial.

48 Learn the Constellations

Constellations are groups of stars that, when linked together, make fascinating shapes in the night sky. The Phoenicians (seafaring European and African travelers) dreamed up the idea to play this connect-the-dots game and give specific names to these star groups some 3,000 years ago. In the 16th century, the Greek astronomer Ptolemy further developed the concept and came up with 48 of the 88 constellations that we commonly know of today. Europeans found the other 40 constellations in the 17th and 18th centuries. Despite some cryptic names (like Equueleus and Centaurus), constellations typically form easy-to-spot images of animals (lions, fish, and crabs) and objects (scales and arrows) if you know where to look. Learning the constellations turns looking at the night sky into a whole new experience. And getting to know them means always being able to impress a date on a late-night country stroll.

How to Do It

Some constellations, such as Ursa Major (the Great Bear), Scorpius (the scorpion), or Orion (the hunter) are visible without a telescope or super-strong binoculars. But barring an unexpected blast-off into outer space to get you up close and personal to Cassiopeia and Pisces Austrinus, the best way to see and learn to identify constellations is through a high-powered telescope. Visit a nearby planetarium to get access to the most advanced magnifying lenses. Star maps are available for download online. Once you establish a few signposts and a sense of interstellar direction, the sky's the limit.

The Big Misconception

Turns out that the Big Dipper, which most people think of as one of the big-time constellations, isn't a constellation after all. It's actually an asterism, a sort of social clique of the seven brightest stars in the Ursa Major constellation.

Constellations and Horoscopes

You may have noticed that the 12 zodiac signs are reflective of nighttime constellations. Why? The same way that countries are located at specific coordinates on lines of latitude and longitude on Earth, stars (and constellations) are located at specific coordinates on lines of right ascension and declination on what astrologists refer to as the celestial sphere. Like lines of longitude and latitude, the coordinates on the celestial sphere are also interpreted in degrees—but they also represent periods of time. (For example, the constellation Scorpious, known as Scorpio in astrology, is located at coordinates that cover a space in the night sky that spans from about October 24 to about November 21.) Everyone's birthday falls somewhere in the night sky and that determines your zodiac sign, which astrologers believe indicates aspects of your personality.

49 Make a Podcast

Everyone and their geeky brother's got a blog these days, and kids who aren't even born yet have social networking pages. If you want to exhibit some digital originality, launch your own podcast. Self-produced "radio" shows that can be recorded as audio files, accessed online, and downloaded onto any iPod, podcasts can be about anything from crossbow hunting to how to care for an unruly pet. You don't need much to get started, just an Internet-equipped computer, a microphone, headphones, audio editing software, and an idea—an original, thought-provoking idea. There are tons of podcasts already out there and, like bad AM radio, the boring ones don't attract very many listeners.

How to Do It

First, consider what you want your show to be about. It could showcase independent hip-hop artists or mixes by the sickest DJs (who just happen to be you and your friends). You can also format your podcast more like a talk show and interview unusual community members like that guy down the block who just got a tattoo on a very sensitive body part. Once you have your idea, come up with a name that captures the spirit of your show and packs a punch (like Motorcycle Diaries: How to Turn Your Clunker Into a Chick Magnet). An outline will give your show some structure and prevent you from "umm-ing" your audience to death, but don't script your whole show or you will sound like that classmate who always gives presentations while reading straight from a piece of paper. Launching your podcast is not technically difficult (hey, grandmas in the Midwest are doing it), but production methods will change depending on whether you have a Mac or a PC. Check out geek sites like *www.engadget.com* and *www.cnet.com* for the how-to.

Soundproof Your Studio

Record in a sound-controlled space, even if it is a bedroom, a bathroom, or that big walk-in closet where your old clothes are stored. Any background noise you might not otherwise hear (like fans, air conditioners, refrigerators, outside traffic, or a computer beeping and humming) will be picked up in your recording and make it hard for listeners to hear what you and your guests are saying.

Are you a pack rat? Do you hold onto birthday cards, movie ticket stubs, love letters, magazine articles, report cards, and other bits of nostalgic ephemera? If your desk is overflowing with mementos of important events—or the "junk box" under your bed is no longer fitting *under* your bed—it's time to get more creative with your organizing. Make an everlasting autobiography by putting everything that represents your interests and activities into a scrapbook. Like a diary or journal, which usually contains your most private thoughts, a scrapbook provides cover-to-cover structure for collecting and preserving the small (and flat) material things that are important to you.

How to Do It

Shop around for a nice blank, about 12- by 12-inch book, that can accommodate a wide variety of stuff. Use light-colored pages if you want to write on them in dark ink, and black pages if you want to use silver or other similarly colored pens. Also pick up rubber cement, tape, and other means of affixing things to the book. Buy stickers, ribbons, and various decorative items to help add flair. When you're ready, sit down at a clean work space with your scrapbook supplies and contents, and begin to put the months' or even years' worth of papers into order. Organize chronologically, so that when you look at the book over time, you can see how your life was influenced by different important events. Also, as you move forward, you'll be able to just add new stuff to the scrapbook's back pages. Think of each page as an individual work of art and experiment by mixing and matching different elements, like photos, play programs, articles from newspapers, and artwork given to you by friends. Label the pages with dates, names, and locations so you'll always know who went with you to the My Chemical Romance concert (write the person's name on the ticket), or how old you were when you had your appendix taken out (that beautiful hospital bracelet — now that's a keeper).

Themed Scrapbooks

If you have tons of stuff and want to organize it by category instead of date, keep a series of scrapbooks, each one dedicated to a particular area of your life — one for school-related stuff, one for crush memorabilia, another for music tickets and concert pics, and so on. You never know — if you reach movie star status someday, these books might be worth something.

51 Make a Video

Love going to the movies, but tired of sitting through lame Adam Sandler comedies, sappy chick flicks, and dull-edged *Saw* rip-offs? Instead of lining up at the multiplex this weekend for yet another overpriced dud, get behind the camera and make your own cinematic masterpiece. Relatively affordable video cameras and easy-to-use editing software are turning today's home-movie amateurs into film festival darlings. (Jonathan Caouette's *Tarnation*, which was made on an iMac for about 200 bucks, was a favorite at Cannes.) And with insanely popular sites like YouTube transmitting bizarre shorts and backyard epics to computer screens throughout the world, your three-minute work of art can be seen by millions of video fanatics looking for creative alternatives to the mainstream crapola churned out by Hollywood studios.

How to Do It

If your family doesn't own a video camera, borrow one from a friend or rent one from a local equipment facility. Familiarize yourself with all the little buttons either by thumbing through a manual or pushing things to see what they do. Make sure you figure out how to use the crucial Zoom button and how to change shooting modes. This way, you can, for instance, choose a widescreen setting for a professional look or black and white for artsy films. (You can also make some of these choices later on in the editing process.) At first, take time to learn technique and don't worry so much about content—you can practice by filming your dog doing stupid pet tricks. Once you've got the basics down, decide what kind of video you want to make. How about shooting a documentary on local musicians or casting friends in a no-budget intergalactic epic? Want to be the next Lonelygirl15? Turn the camera on yourself for an up-close-and-personal confessional (real or fake, it's up to you). Edit your footage into a final cut using iMovie or other software. Hold private screenings of your video at home, or post it on a peer-to-peer site for all to see. But remember: Once something's on the Internet, it's pretty much out of your control. Never publish something scandalous or incriminating. One click of a button can mean months or years of regret. Just ask Paris Hilton.

Spoof for a Goof

Making parodies of an overplayed music video, reality show, or obnoxious TV commercial is a fun way to mess with corporate media. Your satirical interpretation of the latest Justin Bieber video, the TV show *America's Got Talent*, or that mind-numbing SUV ad might just become an online phenomenon.

52 Learn to Match Beats

Back in the day, DJs would cart around back-breaking crates of vinyl records to block, house, and underground parties to spin hours-long continuous mixes custom made for booty shaking. Though some DJs still swear by vinyl, saying it has a greater depth of sound than later digital forms, lots of them also use CDs and MP3s to string songs together—a skill otherwise known as "matching beats." Matching beats is definitely an art (the mixer is an instrument, too—that's how Moby got his start), but it can be learned by anyone with an ear for music and an understanding of simple technology. Once you get the hang of it, you'll be able to keep up the momentum of a party, amp up your social life (everyone loves a great DJ), and share your love of music without saying a word.

How to Do It

You'll need a computer that has separate headphone and speaker out ports, headphones to hear one song, and computer speakers to hear the other. Download a virtual mixer computer program that will help you learn to distinguish beats per minute (BPM) and avoid every DJ's nightmare: the nails-on-a-chalkboard audio trainwreck. You can find a mixer program (some are free, others cost a few bucks) by doing an Internet search for "virtual turntable" or "music mixing program" (be sure to grab one that identifies the BPM for you). Then, pick a couple of MP3s from the same genre of music (they're likely to be close in BPM and easier to mix). Cue the second song at the point in the song where you hear the first drum beat. Then play the first song through the speakers. While it's playing, listen to the second song through one headphone, just like a DJ. (You'll use the program's Cue One and Cue Two buttons to control which song is coming out of the headphone and which is coming out of the speakers.) Next, match the BPMs of the two songs until they are the same (you may need to increase or lower the BPM of the track coming from the headphone to do so). Once the BPM is adjusted —the beats in your headphone match those pouring out of the speakers—use your mouse to slide the cross fader slowly from one side to the other to switch songs. Do it right, and the crowd will yell "Oh-Ohhhhh" when a hot new track feeds into another.

Grandmaster, Cut Faster

Matching beats is fundamental to DJing, but once you've mastered that hurdle, there are so many other things you can do to turn out a seamless mix. Here are two masterly moves:

- Adjust the treble and equalizer on the control panel to make a smoother transition from song to song.

- Scratch records (cut them back and forth across a needle) in order to create repetition and emphasize a killer rhyme.

53 Create a Comic Strip

Way back in the 1950s, adults were convinced that comic books would be the downfall of society. US congressional hearings even cited comic books as a cause for rising juvenile delinquency. The whole country was worried that the violent adventures of Flash, Wonder Woman, and Batman would corrupt impressionable teenagers and distract them from more important things, like doing homework and drinking lots of milk. But today, comic books and cartoon strips are recognized worldwide as important art forms. From classics like *Peanuts* and *Superman* to edgy strips like *Boondocks* to mind-blowing anime from Japan, there's no limit to the crazy characters and wild worlds found in the comics. Taking inspiration from your favorites, create a brand-new comic book or cartoon strip. Who knows, maybe it'll end up in the Sunday paper or on the silver screen some day.

How to Do It

Comics are an ideal format for creative expression—you can choose to make serious social statements, indulge your surreal sense of humor, or reveal personal perspectives on life and how to live it. Once you've decided on a style, come up with a cast of characters to populate your strips. Are they humans, aliens, superheroes, or animals? Or throw all of the above into a fantasy world in which every conceivable creature thrives. Decide if you want to tell your stories in a single panel (like *Dennis the Menace* or *The Family Circus*), or stretch them out into four panels (like *Garfield* and *Blondie*). Once you're comfortable with a format, try to develop a more elaborate storyline that can fill an entire comic book.

Substance Over Style

Don't worry if drawing isn't your strong suit—being funny or charging your comics with unexpected emotion is more important than making everything look lifelike. If you're really struggling with the technical elements, consider partnering with a friend who excels at drawing. He or she can be in charge of the artwork while you focus on character, story, and text.

54 Take an Art Class

Personal expression finds its most poetic outlet in the arts. Given the right tools, training, circumstances, and a willingness to fearlessly explore your artistic potential, you'll find that even stick-figure drawings and macaroni-shell sculptures can reflect deep feelings that are otherwise difficult to express. Taking an art class is a wonderful way to tap into your creative instincts and learn that there's more to art than painting flowers and photographing sunsets.

How to Do It

Sign up for a class at a local art school or community center. You should be able to take a 12-session course for no more than a couple hundred dollars (though you might have to spend extra on supplies). If the enrollment fee is an issue, ask the instructor if scholarships or discounts are available to students—creative types usually aren't so hung up on money, and it's doubtful you'll be turned away. Choose among the offerings, from figure drawing, pottery, and glassblowing to candle-making, photography, and collage, and you're bound to find an artistic medium that jives with your particular style of creativity. Don't worry about getting messy—a little glitter in your hair or green paint on your ripped-up jeans is nothing compared with what some artists have endured in pursuit of their vision.

Show Off Your Accomplishments

Once you've built up a small body of work—like a series of luminous landscape paintings or abstract metal-and-wire sculptures—title the collection and host it as an exhibition. Hold it in a local café, library branch, or even your living room. Title the exhibition to give it further cohesion and prominence. For an extra-professional touch, send out post-cards announcing the show. You can print your own on the cheap at a local copy shop or order them online. Leave stacks at businesses that have a space for flyers or community events postings, like bookshops and music stores, and distribute them at school, work, and parties.

Tired of the pistachio green decor that seemed so cool back when you were in fifth grade? You know your parents will take forever to give your house its much-needed makeover—they've been talking about it since before you were born. So take charge of your own room by painting it a brand-new color, like robin's egg blue, hunter green, burnt orange, or crisp white. Choose a color depending on the mood you're going for: Vibrant colors will brighten your private domain, while pastels will create a relaxing environment. Are you a photographer? Slap on a soft white and turn your room into a gallery ripe for hanging your art. Is your style goth? Represent with a deep purple. It's amazing how different you'll feel when surrounded by colors that relate to your own personality.

How to Do It

Make a deal with your parents: If they spring for the paint and supplies, you'll provide the labor. Then measure the square footage of your room and make a run to the paint store with the checklist on the following page.

- **paint:** 1 gallon is enough for approximately one coat of 250 square feet; flat paint, or the type with eggshell finish, is best for the ceiling and walls, while shinier semigloss paint in an identical or similar color—or white—is ideal for trim

- **spackle:** to plug up holes and cracks in the wall before you paint

- **primer:** necessary if you are covering up a dark color with a light color

- **rollers:** you'll need short ones for the walls and long ones for the ceiling

- **paint trays:** to dip your rollers in

- **paintbrushes:** get a variety of sizes—bigger, flat-tipped ones for walls and smaller, angle-tipped ones for trim

- **plastic drop cloths:** better to buy too many than too few; they can rip, and if you don't have reinforcements that's the end of your floor

- **wide blue painter's tape:** use this to secure drop cloths and to tape around windows, ceiling fixtures, and wall outlets

Also have on hand some rags, sponges, ladders, and small plastic containers to pour paint into so you don't have to dip brushes directly into the can. Once you have all the materials, throw a painting party with your friends! The entire job should take two days tops.

Has the complexity of sheet music kept you from taking music lessons? *Clefs*, *da capos*, and *mezzos* may sound daunting— or at least more like types of lattes than anything related to music—but try not to let the terms deter you. Though it takes a lot of time and effort to learn an instrument, it's actually much easier to pick up basic note-reading and advanced techniques when you're young. And the lifetime rewards of knowing how to toot a trumpet or wail on a harmonica far outweigh the frustrations of your first few lessons.

How to Do It

Decide what instrument you want to learn based on your personality and interests. For example, a trumpet would be great for a deep-breathing yogi. And the guitar is especially useful for songwriters. One-on-one sessions with a virtuoso is one way to go. Check with local music schools and community centers for teachers who prefer to work with beginners. If lessons from the local pros are too pricey, try getting instruction from a college student majoring in music or, even better, from the hottie band member who lives down the street; students will give you cheaper rates than pros and may even be more fun to learn from. Start with one lesson per week, and commit to more training time if your schedule and budget allow. It's best to set specific goals: Do you want to simply learn how to play classic Metallica songs, or are you striving to one day be a professional musician? Regardless, don't get discouraged—even if your early attempts at playing a Mozart concerto or a bluesy White Stripes number make the neighborhood dogs howl.

Instruments to Investigate

If you think the violin and the piano are too mainstream, check out one of these:

- **sousaphone**: a seriously heavy, giant horn that circles around the player's upper body and ends in a big bell that extends above the player's head. It's originally from the US and is mostly played in marching bands.

- **timpani**: an Italian-born copper or brass bowl with calfskin or plastic stretched across its surface. When beaten, it makes a dramatic sound that builds to a big musical climax.

- **zither**: a shallow, armless guitar from Europe that has about 40 strings and is plucked with a pick worn around the thumb. There are lots of different zithers, including the folky dulcimer, which was popularly played in Joan Baez recordings back in the '60s.

57 Take a Dance Class

Sure, you think you're all that when you're alone in your bedroom, blasting Beyoncé or bumping to Lady GaGa. But are you willing to shake what your mama gave you in *public*? The best way to feel footloose and fancy-free next time you step out on the dance floor—whether it be at a party or at the prom—is to take a dance class. They're offered in all sorts of styles, from hip-hop to modern to jazz. Seasoned pros at local dance studios, gyms, or community centers can show you how to shimmy, hustle, bump, grind, and who knows what else. Dancing is a fun way to express yourself and get in touch with your body; it's also great exercise and will make you look and feel like more of a stud than you ever thought possible.

Swing Is the Thing

Hipsters went nuts in the 1930s and 1940s, jitterbugging to big-band tunes, throwing their partners high in the air, and coming up with crazy choreography that still hasn't gone out of style. To bone up on your jump and jive, catch the dance numbers in the movie *Swing Kids* (1993) or see the Marx Brothers flick *A Day at the Races* (1937), which has one of the most influential Lindy Hop sequences ever filmed. Also, check out some classic Cab Calloway or Benny Goodman tunes.

How to Do It

Studios and community centers offer classes for all levels of expertise, from beginner to advanced. Scan the schedule and chat with an instructor to determine which class is right for you. And don't be wary if you're an amateur—in a beginner class, everyone is pretty much on the same page. Plus, a good teacher will be able to teach you what to do with your extra left foot. To prep for class, make sure you wear comfy clothes. Different types of dance require different types of shoes—or no shoes at all—so lace up or lace down accordingly. If practicing in public isn't the thing for you, drop 15 bucks on an instructional DVD. Famous choreographers who have worked with the world's greatest pop stars have released DVDs that break down showstopping moves for the rest of us. With practice, patience, and loosened-up hips, you'll be putting Shakira to shame in no time.

58 Participate in a Performance

Performing in a play can be totally terrifying at first, but there's nothing quite like the thrill of seeing the curtain rise before you and stepping up to center stage for your first big scene. It's an amazing feeling when you slip into character and become someone else for a couple of hours. And don't feel like your only option for drama is the annual school play. High school productions—which tend to feature the same picture-perfect child prodigies or too-polished sopranos year after year—are not the only outlets for budding thespians. Wherever you live, you can find community theaters hungry for a few good teens to take on supporting parts or even juicy lead roles. It's fun to act among adults who know the ropes and how to throw sick cast parties. Whatever role you play—Elphaba in *Wicked*, Hugo in *Bye Bye Birdie*, or Mimi Marquez in *Rent*—you'll discover why they say the neon lights are bright on Broadway.

How to Do It

Attend a few performances at a local theater to familiarize yourself with the venue and recurring cast members. Then sign up to audition for a play. Small theaters are always in search of good actors to fill teen roles (and younger, if you can pass), so there's bound to be a part that's just right for you in at least one of the season's productions. Despite being pulled together without the budget and experience of professionals on the Great White Way (one of Broadway's many nicknames), community theater productions are often polished and provocative. If you get cast, you'll get to experience the rehearsal process firsthand and learn all about drama—on and off the stage.

Behind the Scenes

If you're into theater but don't fancy yourself the next Laurence Olivier or Vanessa Redgrave, get involved behind the scenes. As a volunteer crew member, you can paint scenery, rig the lights, or do costumes or makeup.

59 Write Your Manifesto

If you had to sum up your view on the meaning of life in a five-paragraph essay, what would you write? Never attempted to crystallize your opinions on life, love, work, art, and the mysteries of human behavior in a concise format—a single page that absolutely nails your unique perspective on this crazy, mixed-up world? Now is the perfect time to do it. A manifesto is a statement of belief that can be motivational, caustic, brutally honest, or hilariously satiric. Whatever your approach, a manifesto shines with solid concepts, clever wordplay, and, above all, the writer's intent to sway readers' opinions.

How to Do It

What do you feel strongly about? Are you all pissed off over the cancellation of your favorite sitcom? Explain why in a manifesto aimed at insulting short-sighted TV executives. Or maybe you want to spearhead an "Abolish-Phys Ed" movement, or glorify Lil' Kim's rhyming and wardrobe style. How about a powerful statement on the importance of forming a gay-straight alliance in your community? Pick your topic, shape your opinion and outrage into a tight five-paragraph essay, and distribute the resulting manifesto to anyone willing to read it. You can hand out your diatribe anywhere, but it's best to ask for permission before, say, dropping thousands of copies all over school from an overhead helicopter. Of course, if permission is denied, you can write another manifesto about how much authority figures suck.

Don't Let You Be Misunderstood

As clear and convincing as your manifesto seems
to you, some readers are bound to miss your point
or even feel insulted by your views. Use these
opportunities to create a dialogue around the issue,
and keep an open mind as your detractors have
their say. Maybe Katy Perry's not making such a
badass fashion statement after all.

Look at you, working the vintage Levi's, plaid shirt, studded belt, and beat-up Converse outfit. And that miniskirt with fitted blazer and imitation pearl-drop earrings ensemble? Style points galore. As if you didn't already play dress-up pretty much every day of the year, Halloween is the perfect excuse to fly your fashion freak flag in a daring costume. Instead of shopping for a cheesy getup at the usual Halloween supply store—where your options are limited to "pirate with shoulder parrot," an Incredibles family member, or one of Snow White's dwarves—celebrate the year's spookiest evening by making your own costume. Throwing a white sheet over your head and going as a ghost is scary in all the wrong ways.

How to Do It

Raid thrift stores or your parents' closet for funky cast-offs that will transform you into a disco king, a '50s debutante, or the late great Marie Antoinette. If you're going for a more artsy costume idea, break out the crafting supplies—remnant fabric, body makeup, paints, masks, and props—to turn yourself into anything from the Leaning Tower of Pisa to a slice of pizza. Or come up with a conceptual costume, like a rolling blackout (an all-black outfit and a pair of skates) or a deviled egg (a round oval white costume paired with devil ears and a pitchfork). Challenge yourself to assemble all the costume elements without resorting to premade costume pieces at the mall.

Growing Up Without Ho-ing Up

Somehow, once the trick-or-treating years are gone, big group outings on Halloween turn into big "pimp and ho" fests. You know: underwear as outerwear, fishnet stockings, and faux-chinchilla coats. These costumes show about as much originality as the plastic bunny ones from Wal-Mart. Instead, pick an unusual theme and go partying en masse as a bunch of Hobbits, *Simpsons* characters, or, if you *must* get your tramp on, a few *Desperate Housewives* (at least it shows some creativity).

61 Design a T-Shirt

Why drop 30 bucks or more on a trendy, mass-produced T-shirt that will be worn by everyone you know and then go out of style in two months? Resist the Gapification of America by customizing a crewneck of your own. By making and wearing your own T, you'll stand out in a crowd of Abercrombie & Fitch clones and be recognized as a fashionista worthy of *Project Runway*.

How to Do It

Buy a solid-colored T-shirt; the best deals can be found online or at outlet stores. Just think of the shirt as a blank canvas on which you will create a masterpiece. There are countless techniques for shirt-making. Iron-on decals of retro characters (Smurfs, anyone?) and band logos are fun—center them on the side seam of the shirt to stray from the standard image-across-the-chest look. Or if you're an artist with a message, say it on a shirt with vinyl lettering. You can also embroider the lower corner or shoulder-blade area with a sprawling floral cluster or cut slash marks across the back or sleeves for an '80s effect. And if you have a signature character or doodle you always draw, stamp it on your shirt using a Gocco, or personal silkscreen machine. Anything goes, really—just remember to use paints and markers that are permanent and specifically designed to be washed. And if you screw up, start over. There are always more plain T-shirts to wreak havoc on.

Fit to a "T"

Have a cool design sketched out but prefer to have someone
else do the work? Put "custom T-shirts" into an Internet search
engine to find a slew of online sites that will silk-screen your
artwork onto shirts and send them to you within a couple of
weeks. Also check out *www.threadless.com*. You can buy
affordable, one-of-a-kind shirts designed by hot young artists—
or, better yet, submit a design to the site yourself.

62 Write a Real Letter

Today's teens are lauded for they're multitasking skills. You fire off emails while IM-ing, downloading music, writing a paper, and munching on a bowl of cereal. While pen-on-paper letter writing may seem like an archaic waste of time (you have to form real sentences instead of just plugging in various emoticons), it solidifies your focus and improves your communication skills. The act of writing, rather than typing, is also a slower process in which we tend to pause and thoughtfully consider every word. Not convinced? Here are some other pros.

- You get to send and receive something in the mail (other than another credit card offer).

- You don't have to worry about your message getting hacked into.

- You are creating a tangible keepsake that may even make it into the recipient's scrapbook.

And don't worry, you can still use emoticons—just draw them.

How to Do It

Select stationery that sets the tone of your letter and conveys your mode and intention to the recipient. Quirky Japanese stationery is perfect for expressing thanks to a friend, while crisp white paper (possibly monogrammed with your initials) adds an air of sophistication to business-related letters. Your choice of pen says as much as the words themselves. For full-on old-school effect, use a fountain pen dipped in ink—even the inevitable smudges will appear eloquent. Or just use ink colors outside of the black and blue norm. Handwritten letters work for all kinds of friends. Catch up with your long-lost friend from across the country by sharing recent life events and a couple of snapshots to show what you look like these days. Writing to a loving relative or object of your affection? Scent the letter with a small spray of perfume, and seal the envelope with melted wax.

The Write Stuff

Read over your letter before sending it, checking for egregious spelling mistakes and revealing asides. It's great to be candid and forthright with your letter recipient, but don't get carried away and spill your guts to the wrong person.

63 Write a Letter to Your Future Self

Who you are now indicates so much about who you'll be in the future. Yet as the years pass, some of your current interests and perspectives will fade, and you'll develop new quirks, priorities, and outlooks. That's why it's cool to send a note to your future self. Upon receiving this epistolary surprise sometime in the middle of the 21st century, the grown-up version of you will thank your teenage self for taking an hour or so to put down on paper all your hopes and dreams during your high school years. And you'll be able to reflect deeply on how much you've evolved as time has gone by.

Dark and Dramatized

If you are the nostalgic or introspective type, then looking back on your life through the years is something you probably do often. Have a read of Samuel Beckett's one-act play, *Krapp's Last Tape*. In it, a cynical old man finds diary entries that he had recorded on tape when he was still young. It's a sad but moving play that will definitely lend some inspiration to your own musings.

How to Do It

Using pen and paper, or typing on a computer if you prefer, head your letter "Dear Me" and write down everything you want your adult self to remember about being the age you are right now. What are your favorite school subjects? Who are your best friends and sworn enemies? What are your hobbies, habits, and pop-culture obsessions? Once you've spilled your guts, seal the letter in an envelope and stash it in a box of memorabilia that you will be sure to keep forever (with your yearbooks, for example). Twenty, even ten years from now, you'll find it one day and remember what your junior self was all about and into as a (not-so-) innocent teen.

64 Create a Tasty Dessert

What does whipping up a pound cake or baking oatmeal raisin cookies have to do with personal expression? Ask Sara Lee and Famous Amos. These household names made their mark and plenty of dough (both kinds) by artfully experimenting in the kitchen and coming up with delicious desserts that appeal to billions of snackers world-wide. Even if your oven-bound concoction doesn't wind up in the dessert aisle of every supermarket, you'll definitely score big points with friends (and maybe make some new ones) by sharing your inventive home-baked goods.

Don't Prematurely Preheat

Oftentimes, recipes will instruct you to preheat the oven even before you've collected the ingredients, much less mixed them up. But for first-time bakers, the time it takes to read the recipe, measure, mix, and pour is at least double that of a seasoned baker. To prevent your kitchen from heating up too fast (and to keep it green by saving energy), preheat the oven *after* you've mixed the ingredients. The oven can heat to the right temp while you spoon cookie batter onto sheets, prep cake pans, and clear counter space for your soon-to-be fresh-baked treats.

How to Do It

Almost all desserts include various amounts of flour, sugar, and butter. Scan cookbooks, recipe sites, and the back of food containers (like chocolate chip bags) for hard-to-botch, tried-and-true recipes. If you want to journey off the beaten path, try specialty cookbooks or adding to basic recipes to create your own signature dessert. Experiment with coconut, nutmeg, fruit juice, chutney, olive oil, dried fruits, even ginger — you never know which foods and flavors will mix. Or try healthier substitutions for the standard processed ingredients; agave nectar, which doesn't cause blood sugar levels to spike, can be used instead of granulated sugar, while enriched white flour can be swapped out for whole wheat flour. Accept the fact that you're going to make mistakes as well as a big mess, and build in time for do-overs and a thorough kitchen cleaning at the end of your bake-quake.

65 Volunteer for a Nonprofit Organization

Big businesses like Best Buy and Amazon exist primarily to make money. Sure, they provide consumer services—PlayStations, Linkin Park CDs—but the main goal of mega-companies, banks, law firms, hospitals, restaurants, and gas stations is to take your hard-earned dough and put it in the pockets of high-powered CEOs. Not everyone works for big profit, though. Nonprofit organizations provide social and artistic services like raising money for disadvantaged kids, hosting independent film festivals, representing the needs of various ethnic groups, and finding homes for stray animals. They are often funded by donations, and are less money-driven and more idealistic than regular businesses. Volunteering for a nonprofit is a great way to 1) gain job experience in fund-raising, project management, and public relations, 2) meet interesting people such as community leaders, scientists, and artists, and 3) give back to your community.

How to Do It

Match your interests to a nonprofit org in that field. If you're into anime or manga, contact the local modern art museum and volunteer to lead exhibition tours. Love spending time outdoors? Find out if the local nature conservancy or botanical park needs someone handy with a leaf blower. If you're a math whiz, consider tutoring younger students at a nonprofit education center or afterschool program. Live to swing a hammer? Work with Habitat for Humanity International or another nonprofit that constructs emergency relief housing. Whatever your niche, nonprofits are thrilled to work with volunteers on either a one-time or an ongoing basis. If you choose the latter, establish a schedule with the organization's project manager and stick to it.

Questions to Ask

- What training will you receive?

- Who will supervise your work?

- What perks might you receive as a volunteer (tickets to events, networking ops)?

- If your school agrees, can you receive academic credit for volunteering?

66 Go Green

What do you mean, green isn't your color? Helping to sustain the environment is about the sexiest thing around (well, apart from the Victoria's Secret catalog). The modern-day green scene, started up in the US in the 1980s by former hippies and tree huggers, has grown into a major movement. The point is to change how communities and individuals think about ecology and a range of social issues like ecotourism and biodynamic farming. By "going green," you're pledging to uphold ecological sustainability and social responsibility and putting yourself in the same political camp as Cameron Diaz and Leonardo DiCaprio.

How to Do It

There are so many ways to help out your environment, but these are good ways to start:

1. **Recycle materials.** Paper, cans, bottles, and certain plastics can all be recycled. Recycling means less trash, and saves our overflowing landfills from more than 200 million tons of garbage per year. That equals less land pollution, more open space for parks, less soil and water pollution (which builds up when trash is buried) and less air pollution (which comes when trash is burned). Recycle bins are provided by most city sanitation departments, but when they're not, you can take your recyclables to the nearest recycling center.

2. **Recycle food.** Rather than throw away food scraps, toss them into a compost heap so they turn into usable fertilizer.

3. **Recycle clothes.** Donate your old threads instead of trashing them, and score cool thrift shop finds instead of brand-new clothes.

4. **Buy biodegradable.** Products labeled "biodegradable" will decompose back into the environment.

5. **Recycle bags.** Bring your own shopping bags when you go to stores (most plastic bags are not biodegradeable!).

6. **Reduce energy consumption.** Most of our electrical power comes from coal, which spews carbon dioxide into the environment when it's burned and leads to global warming. Try to reduce your energy consumption by turning off lights when you leave a room and unplugging electrical things (like your cell charger) when not in use.

Green Political Scene

Many countries have a Green Party whose candidates champion environmental sustainability. Here in the US, Green Party candidates have yet to win a presidential election, but in 2010, 18 Green Party candidates in 11 different states won major seats on city councils and school boards, and filled mayoral and other posts.

67 Contribute to Community Beautification

Scientists are a long way off from colonizing Mars, so chances are you're stuck on Earth pretty much forever. Why not do everything you can to keep this amazing but fragile planet as beautiful as possible? You don't have to clean up an entire continent, but you should take pride in your surroundings throughout the neighborhood.

How to Do It

There are countless ways to make your stomping grounds sweeter, without working up a sweat or putting yourself out too much. An obvious place to start is by not throwing stuff like gum wrappers out the car window or tossing empty soda cans in the alley behind school. Beyond that, you can volunteer with your local parks department to plant trees and flowers in sidewalk plots or to slap a new coat of paint on the park's benches. Working with the transportation department, you can adopt a bus shelter as your own, painting and tidying it as needed. Graffiti removal from storefronts is always welcome—talk to the store's owner to arrange a cleanup session. If you'd rather add art to the cityscape, organize a mural painting on a blah exterior wall (just be sure to check in with the shopowner first). Many neighborhoods also feature community gardens tended by a devoted group of green-thumbers who take care of specific plants, fruits, and vegetables that are shared by all.

Change Begins at Home

Feel like your house could use a little beautification? Do what you can to (gently) make your family more aware of their surroundings. Keep your front lawn free of weeds, clear clutter from tables and floors, and persuade your older brother to either fix that nasty broken down car or get it out of the driveway for good.

68 Visit Your Local Officials

You might not be old enough to vote, but as a member of a democratic society you should still get involved in your community by expressing your opinions. Local officials, such as your city's mayor and your district's supervisor, are not elected merely to dine at $1,000-a-plate fund-raiser dinners and make an appearance at the opening of the new mall. They're here to represent the people. So, make an appointment to meet with your town's head honchos. Whether you're eyeing a career in politics or just want to get more involved in community affairs, sharing face time with the bigwigs is a great opportunity to learn more about the inner workings of local government and make your voice heard on issues that affect you and your friends—like raising the minimum wage, reducing the cost of college tuition, or making birth control and safe sex information more accessible at school.

How to Do It

First off, find out who's in charge of what in your local government. For instance, the mayor oversees everything, while supervisors are in charge of specific neighborhoods. Call or visit City Hall to find out who's who, and ask to make an appointment with the official you want to meet. These folks are busy so it may be weeks or even months until you can get in to see them. If you do snag an appointment, it probably won't be for a leisurely sit-down over decaf lattes. Instead, you'll likely be asked to visit the official's office for a 15-minute power meeting. Prepare specific questions in advance about your concern. If a one-on-one appointment is tough to arrange, attend one of the many government meetings open to the public.

People Have the Power

If you can't get an exclusive visit with your legislator, send your thoughts on that political hot topic in writing. For the biggest impact, help motivate friends and classmates to do the same—the more letters and emails you all send, the more attention you'll bring to the issue.

69 Join a Political Campaign

I f you have strong opinions about policies in your community, or country for that matter, you can get more involved by joining a political campaign. Maybe you think that there should (or shouldn't) be a curfew for teens, or that your city should participate only in fair trade practices (a cause often championed by Chris Martin from Coldplay). Even though you may not be able to vote yet, your opinions are important. Volunteering your time and enthusiasm to a campaign and supporting an issue or candidate that stirs your passion puts you smack-dab in the midst of political action and social change. Don't leave all the decision-making and chance for change to older voters. Just because someone has been on the planet longer doesn't make them smarter about what's best for today's society.

Minor Involvement

The minimum voting age is 18, which is a bummer if you're younger and highly opinionated. But even if you're not old enough to vote yet, you can volunteer to serve as a poll worker. Some states have age provisions, so check with your local department of elections for details.

How to Do It

Read up on the candidates running in the next election (they are held every November). Just like in school elections for president, treasurer, and secretary, you'll most likely relate to one of the candidates for mayor or supervisor because their ideas make sense and they seem honest (well, as much as a politician can). Contact campaign head-quarters and announce yourself as a willing volunteer. You can help out by answering phones, stuffing envelopes, and distributing leaflets. On Election Day you'll feel a surge of pride knowing you went out and tried to effect change, even if your candidate doesn't win— this time.

70 Feed the Needy

When we lose power for a few hours or go camping for a few days, we often bemoan the loss of our cable TV or hot morning shower. But there are a great many Americans with a *real* stressor and it's not a lack of cable—it's a lack of food. What can you do about it? Make and deliver food for these people. In most towns and cities, there are programs for feeding the hungry. Churches, shuls, mosques, and other religious organizations generally have something going on. Nonprofit organizations like Food Not Bombs (which promotes sharing free food while protesting war) and The Burrito Project (a national food program initially inspired by the charitable work of San Francisco hip-hop musicians) also get eats to people without funds or kitchens. Ever heard of Meals on Wheels? They assemble and deliver nutritious lunches and dinners to seniors with limited mobility. Choose an organization you like (they all are run differently) and do a little cooking and delivering for them. You'll get to meet some interesting people and feel good about how you spend your free time.

How to Do It

Luckily, you don't have to be a top chef to cook in these programs. All you need is a genuine willingness to help, take directions from the group leader, and keep a regular schedule in which to volunteer (even if it is only a few hours a month). There are probably more community kitchens in your town than you're aware of, as these orgs don't usually have enough money to do major advertising. Decide if you'd like to work with a certain demographic—like homeless families with small children, housebound senior citizens, or teenage runaways. Once you find your place, talk to the program organizer about volunteer opportunities, schedule, and training requirements. Be sure to treat your volunteer work as if it were a paying job. Your boss may not be able to fire you if you skip work, but if you don't show up, people won't eat, which is not cool. By feeding (and getting to know) people less fortunate than yourself, you'll learn a lot about the world that exists beyond your front door, plus make friends with people you otherwise would have never met.

Beyond Christmas

Soup kitchens and other food-delivery programs always get a surge of volunteers around the holidays—too many to even accommodate. It's natural for people to try to help when our culture reminds us it's the right thing do to, but your services are needed more during the rest of the year: summer, spring, and early fall. Then, if you still want to participate in the popular holiday shifts, you'll have a leg up on the guy who walks in off the street looking to help that one day a year.

71 Understand How a Farm Works

Pioneering Americans were just itching to settle on wide open plains, rope their own doggies, and raise their own chuck. But here we are today in a fast-food nation that, for the most part, is clueless about just how food goes from farm to drive-thru window. Visiting a farm is crucial if you want to understand where much of your food comes from, how crops are maintained, and why treating natural resources with respect is essential in this era of global warming and other ecological concerns.

Of course, rural dwellers probably know a thing or two about how much work it takes to get eggs from the henhouse to the table, but for those who think their breakfast is grown in the back rooms of the supermarket, a taste of farm life will bring newfound appreciation for how and why you eat what you do.

How to Do It

Research the nearest farming destination; even if you don't live in the Midwest, there's bound to be at least a few acres of farmland within a few hours' drive or bus ride. Contact the farm in advance—many small farms offer daytrip programs featuring all sorts

of farming ops, from plowing fields with oxen and picking veggies to churning butter and milking Sally (that's the cow). While farming, think about what new skills you can bring back to the city. You won't be able to lay an egg, no matter how hard you try, but you *can* plant an herb garden (see page 88 for pointers) to hang from your windowsill or make a compost pile in your backyard (if you're lucky enough to have one).

A Growing Concern

Everyone's talking about "sustainable agriculture" these days. It's an approach taken by farmers who believe in growing food without harming the environment in the process—that means no chemical dumps or disrupting the ecosystem. But sustainable practices aren't just for farmhands. You can work your own sustainable mojo by replacing your glass cleaner and paper towel with vinegar and newspaper, choosing clothing made from organic materials, and making your own pizza instead of ordering in (to eliminate landfill-bound boxes).

72 Write an Op-Ed

Have strong opinions about what's going on in your community? Want to express your impassioned beliefs beyond the dinner table, where your expertly argued views on politics are ignored in favor of dull debates over the best and worst salad dressing? Reach out to a wide readership by submitting an opinion-editorial, commonly known as an op-ed, to your local newspaper. Most papers devote a page or two each day to these essays written by community members. Have you thought of a great reason why that abandoned lot should be turned into a skate park? Maybe you want your city to host an architectural competition for a monument to soldiers killed in a war? Or maybe you just want to speak out about your views on an international topic of great importance, like finding a cure for AIDS or making peace in the Middle East. The more specific and detailed your op-ed, the better: The point is to spark public dialogue in hopes of bringing people's attention to important issues—and away from nightly sessions of mindless channel surfing.

How to Do It

Check the paper's masthead—that's the list of who's who in the front of the paper—and look for the name of the op-ed page editor. An email address might be provided. If not, phone the editorial department, explain that you'd like to submit a piece, and ask for a contact, as well as guidelines, such as length. To grab attention, lead your op-ed with the most important info and state a persuasive case for why your issue and opinion are important to the local community. Keep your op-ed short and to the point, and respect the other side's point of view while giving strong, factually based reasons for your own. It's pretty much like prepping for a debate at school. Follow up with the editor, who might ask for clarifications or a rewrite before publishing your masterpiece. And keep in mind that not every op-ed submitted to a paper is published—if yours isn't chosen, you can still get your opinion out there by posting the piece on a blog.

Say It in a Drawing

Op-eds also take the form of cartoons. If writing isn't your thing, express your views in pictures. A single-panel cartoon with a pithy caption is worth the proverbial thousand words.

Look around your house—can you believe how much stuff is piled up? It's jamming every closet and cupboard, so that you can never find the one thing you're looking for. Do you really use half of these items? It's time to purge your pad of extras and donate whatever you can to a homeless shelter. This is a great exercise in distinguishing want from need, and the estimated 2-3 million homeless people throughout the US will greatly appreciate your well-maintained castoffs.

New Gift Instead of Thrift

Can you imagine wearing someone else's holey socks? Gross. If you can spare the funds, buy some inexpensive socks, undies, or other personal items and donate them while they are brand new. That way, those who are momentarily down- and-out can enjoy some of the simple comforts we take for granted every day.

How to Do It

Ask family members to go through their closets and set aside items in good condition (no threadbare collars or stained sleeves) that no longer fit or haven't been worn in ages. Coats and sweaters are particularly useful in cold climates. Check bathroom cabinets for unopened bottles of shampoo, tubes of toothpaste, and other essential toiletries that you've purchased in bulk. Blankets and pillows are always needed, as are diapers, children's toys, batteries, and paperback books. Gather everything together in boxes—make sure they're not too heavy—and call a local shelter to arrange for delivery. Organizations such as Goodwill and The Salvation Army will often pick up boxes from your home—but don't expect them to take ratty old couches or torn mittens off your hands. They can only use items in good shape. Save the organizations some time by separating the good stuff from the junk and throwing out the junk (or recycling it, when possible) yourself.

74 Raise Money for a Charity

As you may already know, doing the right thing in your community is often about sweat equity, meaning that your volunteer time, friendliness, enthusiasm, and donation of services and goods to a worthwhile cause are just as important as contributing cash. Sometimes, though, it takes dollars—and lots of them—to bring swift assistance to those in need. Raising money for a charity or disaster relief takes persistence and persuasiveness, but if you feel truly passionate about the cause, your urgency will convince like-minded philanthropists and cheapskate skeptics to fork over a little cash.

How to Do It

Identify a charity whose mission moves you. Maybe you know someone with diabetes, cancer, or another illness that requires research dollars and preventative care outreach. Or maybe there's a timely cause—a natural disaster has wreaked havoc on a city, or the local children's theater is in danger of closing due to a rent hike. Whatever your pet cause, work with a representative from the organization to help raise some funds. Decide on a target amount—this will help the group push to meet the goal—and then recruit fellow do-gooders to help with the cause. You can put on a car wash, a battle of the bands, or an open mic night and charge a cover or take donations at the door. Other ways for young people to raise money are by organizing silent auctions, a bingo or poker night, or the tried-and-true bake sale. If you'd rather raise funds without getting caught up in time-zapping organizational work, join a walk, bike or run for your favorite cause and solicit donations from your friends and family. It's essential to be creative with fundraising—it makes it more fun for everyone, and it makes raking in cash a lot easier.

Think Global, Act Local

Disasters such as Hurricane Katrina, which affected Louisiana and Mississippi, and the tsunami that devastated Southeast Asia cause unbelievable damage totaling in the billions. Folks in areas that are hit by sizeable natural disasters need all the help they can get for years afterward. Head up a local fundraiser for disaster relief for one of these places (or another that you know of), and send the collected amount as a gift from your entire town.

Some of you are already all over this. Lots of kids start working somewhere, somehow in middle school. But if you're just cruising through high school without knowing the joys (and, yes, sometimes agony) of being employed, you're missing out. Sure, you're busy with school, blog reading, and soccer practice, but setting aside a few hours a week for work is definitely doable. Even if you don't need the money (though, who doesn't?), working has a lot of benefits. It gives you confidence, independence, a competitive edge when you're applying for college, and something to put on a résumé when you really do need to start looking for a job. It also gives you a sense of accomplishment that far surpasses reaching level 62 on *Prince of Persia*.

How to Do It

Scout out your favorite shops, restaurants, and organizations for "help wanted" signs. Inquire about openings even when you don't see a sign, especially if there is a place you'd really like to work. If you're eager enough, a busy employer may hire you anyway. You'll need to fill out an application with contact info and work history (with start and end dates), so it's helpful to bring with you a premade cheat sheet to complete applications on the fly. Also drop off your résumé (see page 164), if you have one. And don't worry if you have little or no prior experience—entry-level positions are usually designed for newbies. If your school has career advisers, check in with them, too. They probably keep a list of more unique job openings that are perfect for students (part-time gymnastics coach, anyone?) Persistence pays off—call or visit your prospective employer one week after applying if you haven't yet heard back. You'll stand out as ambitious and proactive, and will beat out those slackers who submit sloppy applications and don't follow up.

Adventures in Babysitting

If you are not already watching your younger siblings for free (or even if you are), a paid babysitting gig is a great way to get started in the world of working. Sure, dirty diapers are an odorific fact of life that most people would rather not deal with, but there are lots of other aspects of baby-watching (witnessing little Leo try to walk is serious entertainment) that make it worth it. For your first few adventures, babysit for a close relative who will be more forgiving if they have to be called home to handle Justin's or Jasmine's endless screaming spree.

76 Write a Résumé

Some after-school jobs are easy to come by—a neighbor asks you to babysit or your dad's friend hires you to help at his shop because he, well, knows your dad. But unless you're ridiculously lucky, you won't get every job based on connections alone. To fight for the most coveted positions out there, like resident indie expert at the record store or commision-earning salesperson at the new upscale boutique, you need to be armed ... with a résumé. This page-long personal stats sheet not only gives you a chance to flaunt your specialized knowledge, skills, and education, but also sends the vital I've-got-my-shiznit-to-gether message to potential employers, showing them you're organized, motivated, and serious about working for them. Oftentimes, a manager won't be able to meet your dazzling self when you've chosen to drop by, but if you drop off a killer résumé, she can read it later and call you for an interview. Résumés are also essential for internships, scholarships, and even volunteer positions. Mastering the art of writing job-landing prose will help you secure big opportunities down the road—and steer you away from the yeah-whatever-i-guess-I'll-take-it gigs in the meantime.

Cover Your Butt

One of the most essential parts of a résumé isn't the résumé at all—it's the cover letter. When applying for more serious jobs, include a brief, two-paragraph cover letter that shows optimism and enthusiasm, and explains why you are perfect for the job. It's a necessity for more full-time jobs down the line and will show your prospective employer that, even working part-time, you mean business.

How to Do It

To start, look at some other résumés. If you have an older sibling or friend, hit him or her up for a quick lesson. Your English teacher can also point you in the right direction—either with an after-school tutorial or a good book with some prime examples. To begin your résumé, put your name and all of your contact info at the top. Then, write a one-sentence job goal that highlights your strongest skill, such as, "To contribute my shopping expertise and enthusiasm to the retail sector." After that, make a date-ordered list (most recent first) of all your prior work experience (yes, babysitting and working for your parents' business counts). List the duties you had at each job, using sophisticated language, like "tendered cash" as opposed to "rang people up at the register," and "assisted in administrative duties, such as filing" instead of "put files in order." Add in sections for extra-curricular activities, especially things that show leadership (captain of the debate team, choreographer of the dance squad), special skills (language, computer, interpersonal), and references (use teachers and past employers, not your friends or parents). Finally, make sure the résumé is cleanly formatted, easy to read, spell-checked, and printed on attractive, *colorless* paper. (If pink résumé paper didn't work for Elle Woods in *Legally Blonde*, it's probably not going to work for you.) And remember that job-searching is a lifelong quest. So don't delete your résumé after you've landed a gig. Keep a copy of the master file handy, and modify it as your work and life experience grows.

77 Make and Follow a Budget

If you have a job—or very generous parents—you have some money coming in. Even if you are forced to use some of it on necessities, you probably have at least a little left over to spend on yourself. Rather than blow it *all* on one pricey video game or pair of designer shoes, you're better off parceling out your hard-earned dough into specific categories and keeping track of how, when, and where you spend. That means making a budget. Initially, developing a budget may seem like a homework assignment for econ (so maybe not a thrill a minute). But you can actually learn a lot about yourself by creating a list, or table, of all the things you spend money on (like food, entertainment, gas, public transportation, and school supplies). By laying it all out in front of you, you can see what your financial needs and desires are and learn to prioritize—so you spend less money on stuff you *don't* really need or want and more money on stuff you *do*.

How to Do It

You don't need to have an MBA to make a budget—you just need to know how to make a spreadsheet. Either on paper or in a computer program like Excel, list everything you spend money on throughout a typical month. Include school supplies, clothes, movies, snacks, sporting equipment, magazine subscriptions, online memberships, and anything else you toss cash at. Assign a maximum weekly dollar amount to each category. At the end of the week, add up how much you've spent in each category and compare the total to your maximum amount. Are you over your limit in clothes but under in movies? Maybe you need to adjust your budget so it's more in line with your spending habits or financial limitations. In any case, try to meet or spend less than your total monthly max. Establish reasonable spending and saving patterns, and you'll feel better about splurging on front-row tix to that Black Eyed Peas concert.

Choose Not to Charge

Sure, celebs may look totally happy in major credit card commercials when shown spending their lives away. But *they* can afford to pay off huge credit card bills every month. The rest of us can't. Credit card companies specifically target teens through advertising, knowing that people in your age group are tempted to take a new Visa or MasterCard on a no-holds-barred shopping spree. Don't let them get you. It's easy to "charge it" now, but when big balances and interest pile up it's a lot harder to pay it off later. If you're not careful, you can get yourself into a mess that your parents won't be so thrilled to bail you out of. Besides, owing other people is a drag. Be smart and just use a debit card or cash.

78 Open a Savings Account

You're certainly entitled to spend hard-earned dough on high-end jeans, iTunes downloads, limited-edition kicks, and other bling, but it's never too early to start saving. Hip-hop icon Ludacris made his millions by releasing his albums independently. That way, he kept all the profits without having to share with the record companies. How did he do it? He had enough of his own cash to start his business. So, how much have you got hidden under the mattress? If the answer is zilch, it's time to open a bank account and start saving for college tuition, a car, and other big-ticket items that will allow you to invest in yourself and make your dreams a reality.

The Zen of 10

Try to put away at least 10 to 15 dollars every month—that's just one less night at the movies or extra-large pineapple pizza. With a few bucks in the bank, you'll feel more like a high roller, less reliant on your folks, and free to call your own shots. (Think Donald Trump ... but with better hair.)

How to Do It

Remember that goofy piggy bank you got from Aunt Ethel for your eighth birthday? Bust it open, count your coins, and march down to the bank to open a savings account. Many banks offer special deals for teens who are opening their first account, so ask a teller to explain the options, and make sure your nest egg earns a decent interest rate. Just about every bank has a website, so you can log on to keep track of your savings.

79 Understand the Stock Market

Buy low. Sell high. Diversify your portfolio by dumping those risky hedge funds and opting instead for a blue chip mutual fund. Huh? Stock market terminology and financial data are like a foreign language at first—you have to study and practice it to understand it. But with time and devotion, you can learn the lingo well enough to play the game—and hopefully win. The stock market, which has a long history in the US and even longer abroad, is perhaps the world's biggest casino (you have to be 18 to participate, but you can start learning about it sooner).

To play the market, people buy different types of investments such as stocks, which are actually small portions of a company. If the company with which you bought the stock does

Put Your Money Where Your Mind Is

To learn all the ins and outs of buying low, selling high, and coming out ahead, pick up these top reads.

- *Standard and Poor's Guide to Money and Investing:* gives you a soup-to-nuts understanding of the financial market

- *The Warren Buffett Way*: a book about the investment strategies of a world-famous stock market genius

- *Stock Investing for Dummies*: an intro to investing in the stock market for newbies

well during the year, you generally make money. If that company does poorly (or worse, goes out of business), then you're in trouble. Experienced investors usually know the right strategy for investing and when to buy and sell. That being said, the market is unpredictable, and even the best "gamblers" sometimes lose a bundle. At some point you'll have a few hundred or thousand to spare, and having a better idea of how to invest it will save you from losing your shirt. Of course, playing the stock market is always a bit risky—never invest money that you cannot live without.

How to Do It

The best way to begin to understand the stock market is to pick a few stocks to follow and chart their ups and downs over a period of three to six months. To do this, go to the finance sections of major websites such as *www.finance.yahoo.com* or *www.moneycentral.msn.com*. Pick companies you like and believe in, or new ones you want to learn about, and track their stocks' progress on a spreadsheet. To better understand why the stocks fluctuate, check out the latest news on the companies (maybe they announce a merger or roll out a new product) and see how recent developments affect the stock prices. You can also check out the *Wall Street Journal* and *Fortune* magazine for more in-depth coverage. By the time you're able to legally participate in the game, you'll have a basic idea of how to play.

80 Take Care of a Pet

When it comes to companionship, reliability, and emotional support, animals offer distinct advantages over humans: They listen attentively as you complain about your geometry teacher, they stick to a predictable routine of eating, sleeping, playing, and pooping, and they provide unconditional love as long as you scratch their tummies and reward their obedience with gross-smelling treats. Taking care of a pet is also a great way to learn how to be responsible for another living creature, and your very own Garfield, Snoopy, or Stuart will teach you much about the importance of dependability and loyalty. Just be sure you're ready for the commitment before approaching Mom and Dad about that "adorable puppy"—after all, your parents are not going to be the ones cleaning up Spot's less-than-adorable mess.

How to Do It

Carefully consider the size of your living space and your amount of available time. Dogs take up plenty of room, are hands-on, and require early morning walks and plenty of exercise, while cats are more independent and like to pretend they don't really need you once they've outgrown the ball-of-string phase. Cost is a factor, too, and goldfish or hamsters are perfect if you don't want to spend too much on your pet's upkeep. Whether you adopt a floppy-eared puppy with a bark-worse-than-bite complex, a slinky feline with don't-bother-me eyes, or a bashful turtle with intimacy issues, your pet will have a distinct personality that you'll need to nurture or modify through training. Take cues from TV's famous dog whisperer, Cesar Millan, or similarly wise pet experts. And if you are absolutely not allowed to have an animal in the house because of family-member allergies or distaste for things not human, get acquainted with a neighbor's pet or volunteer at a local shelter for a few hours a week.

Co-op Your pet

If you're jonesing for some puppy love but are worried your schedule won't allow you to keep up with Fido's needs, ask a family member to join you in taking ownership of a new dog. Sure, you might have to compromise on which breed to get and what to name it, but snagging an accomplice will cut dog-walking duties in half and give you more freedom to hang with friends after school.

81 Take Care of a Houseplant

Want to take care of a living thing, but not one that barks all night, pees on your homework, or requires a toilet-flushing funeral? A friendly houseplant will spruce up your stuffy bedroom with verdant color and leafy ambiance. By taking in carbon dioxide and giving off oxygen, indoor plants clean your environment while lending jungle chic to your desktops and nightstands. Name your plant and develop a relationship with it—and watch as your new friend thrives under your care.

Cocktails With Your Cactus?

In his 1848 book *The Soul-Life of Plants*, German physicist and philosopher Gustav Theodor Fechner promoted the idea of talking to plants to aid their growth, believing that greenery responds to emotion. While this theory has never been proven, there's certainly no harm in yakking to your Fishtail Palm about last week's episode of *Saturday Night Live*.

How to Do It

First, pick a plant. Ficus trees, lithops, begonias, African violets, coleus, pothos, ferns, parlor maples, and bamboo all tend to grow well indoors, and you don't need much of a green thumb to keep them healthy and happy. Plants from the succulent family, including the soothing cure-all aloe vera and exotic cacti, are a breeze to nurture (they don't need much water), but their sharp tips can be a pain in the butt—or, more likely, finger. Intensely colored bromeliads require just the right amount of water and light but are well worth the effort—they'll transform your bedroom into a tropical paradise. Ask a horticulturist (also known as the plant store person) for the right sort of potting soil and food. And be sure to find out how much or little light and water your weeping fig or Chinese evergreen needs, as under- or over-watering is the chief cause of premature demise.

After years of suffering the humiliation of having a parent or older sibling drive you, your friends, and maybe even your date (ouch!) around in a rusty old station wagon, you're probably gunning to get a driver's license. There's nothing quite like putting the pedal to the metal—even if the "metal" is the floor of your mom's rickety Dodge Caravan. Getting your license and driving on your own? Now that's freedom, baby! But as Peter Parker would remind you, "With great power comes great responsibility." When you're behind the wheel, you're responsible for the lives of everyone in the car and on the road (even the losers who cut you off). As long as you follow the rules of the road and don't abuse the privilege, driving will take you into your future with style, speed, and hopefully a minimum of breakdowns and flat tires.

How to Do It

Rules and regulations differ from state to state, but in general it's best to start by taking a driver's education course, either at school, or at a private training center. You'll learn the ins and outs of the wide open road (and those narrow city streets) and get to go behind the wheel with an approved trainer who generally has a second brake on the right side (to prevent you from totaling the crappy little Ford Escort you're practicing with). While learning, it's best to start in a big, empty parking lot, gingerly working up to roads, main boulevards, and, when you're ready, multi-lane highways. When you take your driving test at the DMV, don't be bummed out if you fail the first or second time—it's really common. This is one test you absolutely want to ace, so just keep studying and practicing until you're completely comfortable whipping through traffic and cutting those three-point turns.

That Super-Important Life-Altering Phone Call Can Wait

Car accidents are terrible and traumatizing, even when they are small, and often they aren't. Don't jeopardize your safety—and the safety of others—just because you had to share a new pic from your camera phone with your best friend. Turn off your cell phone before you even start the engine, so you won't be distracted from making a tricky left turn when your Gwen Stefani ringtone suddenly starts singing "Crash."

83 Learn Basic Car Maintenance

Whether you've recently gotten your license or prefer to ride shotgun while a friend does the driving, so that you can play DJ, it's crucial that you learn the basics of car maintenance. Changing a tire isn't as tough as it looks, and checking tire pressure, oil, windshield wiper fluid, and brake fluid levels is as easy as pumping gas (if you don't know how to do that, you better learn fast). You don't have to be a full-on grease monkey or scooch under the chassis to check out your auto's innards, but you'll keep the car, and yourself, in better shape once you master the basics. Being prepared on the road instills confidence and security—and prevents you from having to thumb it back to town.

How to Do It

Ask a friend or family member who knows something about cars to give you a 101 on what's happening under the hood. It's best to go to someone who can teach you what to do without being condescending. You'll want to identify:

- **the battery:** a big black box with two knobs—red and black—protruding from the top

- **the engine:** usually the biggest hunk of metal under the hood

- **the oil tank:** the reservoir with a dipstick, usually marked "oil"—be careful, some cars have a separate dipstick to check transmission fluid

- **the coolant:** the atomic-green colored stuff

- **the main fuse relay box:** a black box under the hood, usually marked as such

Play connect the dots and ask your car-friendly tutor to explain how the hunk of junk gets going when you turn the key in the ignition and tap the gas pedal. Also get some quick tips on how to check the oil and other fluids (some should be checked after the engine has warmed up, while others—like the oil—should be checked when the engine is cool), adjust the tire pressure, and jump-start a battery with cables. Next, be sure to outfit the trunk with a spare tire, a tire jack, a quart or two of oil, a gas can, jumper cables, and emergency flares. Don't forget a rag to wipe the oil dipstick, and a tire gauge to check the pressure.

Run Smoothly

Take your high school hot rod (or '95 hooptie) into a mechanic every three months or 3,000 miles (whichever comes first) for a routine oil change. This takes only a few minutes (unless there is a wait) and can be done at your regular mechanic or at a special quick-lube type of place.

84 Assemble a Toolbox

Handy with a hammer? Or screwy with a screwdriver? Whether you're a fix-it pro or kinda clueless when it comes to household repairs, it's a good idea to outfit a toolbox with a dozen or so essential items and learn how to use them all. There's probably someone in your life right now on whom you always depend to fix stuff. Learning how to do it yourself creates less reliance on an outside party, which means you can get things done when and how you want them.

Keep 'Em Clean

Keep tools clean and dry because dirt and water will rust them. Machine oil is an effective cleaner, and steel wool will polish them up like new. Add a can of WD-40 to your kit, and give all the tools a thorough going-over every few times you use them.

How to Do It

Head to a nearby hardware store and peruse the goods, familiarizing yourself with different kinds of tools. Ask for assistance if you're not sure what certain tools are for. A basic toolkit should contain:

- hammer

- pliers

- wrench

- large and small screwdrivers (both standard and Phillips head)

- cordless drill with a set of bits

- utility knife

- level

- assorted nails and screws

- tape measure

- gloves

- safety goggles

- flashlight

These should get you started on tasks such as hanging a picture frame, cutting speaker wire, and assembling Ikea-type furniture. As your skills advance, add specialty items to the toolbox. If you have enough cash, pay a bit more for better-quality tools—they'll last for decades.

85 Learn Basic Clothes Maintenance

If you haven't already, it's time to discover what happens to your clothes between the time they get tossed into the hamper (if they make it that far) and land freshly washed and neatly folded on your bed. Sadly, there's no laundry law stating that Mom, Dad, or the housekeeper should clean your stinky, mysteriously stained clothes for eternity. If you're already washing your clothes, pat yourself on your fresh-smelling back. If not, "laundry" doesn't have to be a dirty word. Just gather up your faded jeans, favorite hoodie, and funky socks, and get the spin cycle going. While you're at it, learn some other aspects of basic clothes maintenance, too, like ironing, sewing buttons, and hemming pants or skirts. Doing your own laundry comes with more benefits than just parental approval; it prevents other people from shrinking your favorite T-shirt down to Barbie doll size, going through your pockets, or mistakenly bleaching your dark-blue denims until they're no longer dark … or blue.

How to Do It

Separate your whites and colors. Wash whites in hot water, which is best for getting out gross stains; wash colors in cold, so they won't fade or run. If you spilled salad dressing on your favorite jeans or cut yourself shaving and got blood on your collar, you may need to use some stain remover. (Let the stain remover soak in for a bit before washing.) If you don't want certain clothing items to fade or shrink, you're better off hang-drying them than tossing them into the dryer. Delicate items such as wool sweaters, lingerie, and linen pants should be washed separately on a delicate cycle or, better yet, by hand in the sink, and laid flat to dry. Check the lids of the washing machine and dryer for cycle, time, and temperature instructions. Fold your clothes as soon as they're dry or they may end up looking like you've slept in them. Some items will need to be ironed anyway—ask your in-house laundry master for a tutorial or see the below tip for a shortcut.

Use Eco-Friendly Detergent

While most traditional detergents are high in chemicals that can irritate skin and eyes, eco-friendly detergents are generally made with biodegradable, nonpetroleum-based chemicals that cause fewer allergies. Also, because eco-friendly laundry suds are nontoxic, you can re-use the water you washed your clothes in to safely water your lawn.

Steam Press on the Go

Don't have time to iron? Take your wrinkled clothes with you into the bathroom when you shower. Hang them on the back of the door or lay them on a flat surface. Then shower with the door closed. The hot steam produced from the shower will take the wrinkles (at least most of them) out of your clothes.

86 Learn CPR

The heart is a resilient muscle built to withstand crushing breakups, fatty foods, and cheesy Valentine's Day cards. But sometimes, when pushed to the max, it says, "Enough!" When someone's heart quits, it can be fatal. Many times, however, you can help save a person who is undergoing cardiac arrest (the medical term for a heart attack) by performing cardiopulmonary resuscitation, also known as CPR.

Make a Splash

CPR can also be used to save the life of a drowning victim (once they are out of the water). If you've mastered CPR and are also an experienced swimmer who loves hanging out at the beach or community swimming pool, consider becoming a lifeguard. The American Red Cross and local safety organizations train lifeguards. You have to be at least 15 years old and devote 30 to 40 hours to learning rescue skills. What a cool job—you get to save lives *and* hang out on the beach or at the pool all summer.

How to Do It

CPR training is available free of charge at professional, volunteer, and government organizations in nearly every city, and you can also pay to take a course. Check out *www.learncpr.org* and *www. redcross.org* to find out where classes are held. In your three-hour course, you'll learn how to quickly assess a victim's condition and apply these life-saving procedures, which consist of mouth-to-mouth resuscitation (breathing air into the victim's lungs) and performing chest compressions. The point of mouth-to-mouth (you'll practice on a mannequin, so no need to worry about the garlic you ate for lunch) is to keep oxygen flowing into the blood via the lungs; the chest compressions are intended to keep the blood flowing, especially to the brain. Remember, however, that CPR is only a *first step*; it is used to buy some time before a medical professional arrives to restore the victim's heartbeat, usually by using an automated external defibrillator. That means it is *absolutely essential* to call 911 as soon as the incident occurs. Then practice CPR while you wait for help.

87 Be Prepared for an Emergency

From earthquakes on the West Coast to hurricanes in the South to tornadoes in the Midwest, nature loves to humble us with mega disasters that are freaky to think about and even worse to go through. It's impossible to predict if and when you might be caught up in a natural catastrophe—but it's possible to lessen the impact by being prepared. Rather than stress out all the time about the unknown, take a single day to organize essential provisions and learn some simple procedures around the house. Then do your best to let go of the worry. You'll be as prepared as you can be should a major situation arise.

How to Do It

To be prepared, take the following practice.

- Gather with your family and go through the house together, making sure that everyone knows how to turn off the gas, switch on circuit breakers, and change fuses.

- Store extra fuses in a utility drawer or cabinet, along with lightbulbs, flashlights, batteries, candles, and matches.

- Program numbers for the police, fire department, paramedics, and family doctors into everyone's cell phones.

- Know the location of the nearest emergency room—you might need to take a loved one there for treatment.

- Buy a first-aid kit, or put together your own with items bought at a drug store. Include bandages, antibiotic ointment, aspirin, bottled water, and medications taken by anyone in the family. Keep the first-aid kit with your emergency supplies.

- Make sure you have plenty of bottled water on hand in case the tap water supply is tainted, and stock up on nonperishable food that doesn't have to be heated (pineapple chunks, peanut butter, baked beans) and a sturdy can opener, so you'll have plenty to eat if cooking with gas or fire isn't possible. Don't forget food for your pets.

- Assemble a "grab and go" backpack that includes extra clothes, some food, and emergency items (like those listed above) that you can grab and take with you in a hurry.

Be a NERT

That's NERT, not nerd. NERT (Neighborhood Emergency Response Team) is a nationwide training program that teaches you how to handle various crisis situations, from house fires to earthquakes. Find out more online by entering your city name and "NERT" into any search engine.

88 Try a New Hairstyle

Creative coiffing is not just for those gel-happy neo-punks or bed-headed glamazons who change their hair color every Thursday (you know who you are). If you've had the same cut for ages, you're probably so used to your old style that you don't realize it's gone from hairdo to hair don't. Buzzcuts and chronic ponytails are like a disease that needs to be cured. Why not try something new? Experiment with different styles, cuts, colors, and products. What's the worst that can happen? Well ... try not to worry about that. Entrust your tresses to an adventurous expert at the barbershop or beauty salon. And if things go awry, just keep repeating: It'll grow back, it'll grow back. And maybe invest in a hat.

Hair to Dye For

Planning to dye your mop bright pink or aquamarine? Use only the best products that won't damage your hair. And if your school or employer has a dress code, make sure they're OK with radical colors and cuts before you do anything drastic. As for what your parents will say ... well, you're on your own with that one.

How to Do It

Browse through magazines and surf the web in search of trendy styles or classic cuts that look appealing and easy to maintain. Celebs constantly show off new looks—study what works well on them and adapt their designer looks to fit your own style and budget. Discuss various options with your barber or stylist that are totally different from your current cut. Do you hide behind your hair? Then cut those eye-obscuring bangs. Do you spend hours taming your unruly locks with relaxers and a straightening iron? Tone down the upkeep by going au naturel, growing dreads, or getting braids. Guys who are way overdue for a hair-cut should take a chance on a messy faux hawk. For those with tight, curly locks, go for volume instead of length and kink it into

a'fro. Or channel Snoop Dogg or Bo Derek with a tight head of cornrows. And then, in a few months, change it up again.

89 Confess a Crush

You've been staring at your latest love from across the school cafeteria at lunch for weeks or even months, trying to work up the nerve to make your move but always coming up with great reasons why today is not the day. Then when he or she walks by, your stomach flip-flops, you turn beet red, and start to sweat. A moment later, you're kicking yourself for not trying to squeak out a simple "hi." Crushes are like too much candy—they make you feel hyper and giddy and then sort of sick and exhausted from the sugar crash. The only way to get over these symptoms is with a confession. You'll never know how he or she feels until you declare your undying love (or temporary like). So muster every ounce of self-esteem you've got and get ready to approach the object of your affection.

How to Do It

You can spend the rest of your life planning the perfect opening line, which you'll most likely blow anyway, or you can be spontaneous and rely on your natural charm to carry you through the first few potentially awkward moments. Either way, break the ice with a brief intro—your name and something about where you've seen each other before, maybe in a class or at the community pool. Chat about school, mutual friends, and the upcoming weekend's game or concert. If you get the cold shoulder, back off, and try again another day, when the mood or surroundings are more conducive to flirtatious banter. If all goes well, stay calm and keep the conversation going. If you get smiles a lot and some flirting back, that's your cue to ask him or her out on a date.

Breathe Easy

The last thing you want to do is scare off your potential date with the breath of death. Keep mints handy and pop one before popping the big question—"Wanna hang out sometime?"

90 Tell Someone Your Darkest Secret

Have you done something so sinful, stupid, or just plain strange that it's keeping you awake at night from excitement, embarrassment, or fear? Is there a skeleton in your closet whose rattling bones remind you of a one-time mistake or ongoing transgression? While many personal activities can and should remain private—revealed only to the pages of your diary—some deeds deserve to be shared with a confidant. So, whether you have a crush on your best friend's girlfriend, shoplifted makeup from Target, cheated on your history final, or like to dress up in drag, unburden your conscience by confessing your deepest, darkest secret.

How to Do It

First of all, if you've done something seriously illegal, or are participating in an activity that is dangerous to you or others, it's crucial that you talk to your parents, guidance counselor, or another adult who can help you before the situation gets any further out of control. That being said, if your secret isn't jeopardizing your health or leading to your appearance on *America's Most Wanted*, then spill the beans to your BFF, a close sibling, a coach you connect with, a family friend, your doctor—anyone who you know you can trust not to betray your confidence. Once the words are out of your mouth, you'll most likely feel a strong sense of relief. Discuss the situation with your confidant and calmly decide what, if anything, you need to do next.

Online and Anonymous

If you really want to confess your secret but can't bring yourself to tell anyone face-to-face, there are websites where you can anonymously submit your wrongdoing or personal quirk—and read those of others.

91 Go Skinny-Dipping

C'mon, admit it: You've always wanted to do this. It's a completely understandable instinct. Being immersed from head to toe in fresh water, sans clothing, is an incredible feeling—after all, you started life in a similar state, surrounded by water while in the womb. There's nothing harmful about skinny-dipping, as long as you don't expose yourself inappropriately or confuse natural nakedness with sexual stirrings. While skinny-dipping can be an intimate and sensual experience, it's more about getting in touch with nature and honoring your body in its unadorned state than it is about a *Girls/Guys Gone Wild* audition.

How to Do It

The best thing to do is to get together a group of friends (same gender!—it's hard to relax when you're conscious of being checked out or creeped out by exes or potential mates) and devote an afternoon to a clothes-free swim. The most challenging part of skinny-dipping is shucking off your modesty, but that's also the whole point. Baring all in front of friends is a great way to get over your societally imposed body issues and feel comfortable in your own skin. If you really hate the idea of stripping down in front of your pals, you can also go it alone. Either way, don't just unhook and unbutton any old place. Try and find a secluded but safe place where you won't be stared at and your clothes won't be stolen. It's cool to do it in your backyard swimming pool, or that of your friend, but just make sure everyone in proximity is OK with a clothing-optional policy. As for public beaches and ponds, skinny-dipping is appropriate only when these sites expressly permit it. Swimming or sunning in the buff where it's not legally allowed might earn you a hefty fine for public indecency (but only the most uptight cops or park rangers would dream of hauling you to jail for a harmless dip).

Did You Know?

The term "skinny dipping" was first used in English in the 1960s. Previously, nude bathers sometimes were referred to as "going starkers." By the way, "skinny" here refers only to your skin and has nothing to do with weight. Bodies of all shapes and sizes should enjoy a suitless soak.

92 Get an Astrology Reading

Saturn is in the sixth house, the moon is waxing, and celestial bodies are lining up across the night sky. Believers in astrology will interpret these seemingly random cosmological conditions as undisputable evidence of one's state of health or impending romantic bliss. For eons, superstitious stargazers have attempted to explain the mysteries of life and the meanings of human behavior by linking the position of the planets to birthdays and personal fates. Every star sign has its own mythology, characteristics, and symbolic animal or archetype—Capricorns are goal-oriented goats, Taureans are headstrong bulls, Aquarians are idealistic water-bearers, and so on. Ultra-rational types insist that there's no truth to the astrological system, while zodiac followers won't make a move before consulting their horoscope. Are you a skeptical Scorpion or a progressive Pisces? Regardless of your sign or belief system, it's fun to indulge the cosmos by consulting with an astrologer.

How to Do It

Even the smallest towns have resident astrologers. Make an appointment with a reputable one—check references and confirm a price before committing to a session. During your meeting, the astrologer will ask when you were born and some questions about your family, school, love life, and future goals. Based on this info and an intuitive sense of your personality, the star seer will create a customized astrological chart for you. The chart is a big circle with lots of lines running through it. The chart's southern hemisphere relates to your external life, while the northern hemisphere deals with your inner life. Signs of the zodiac are placed

around the circle, each linked to traits, parts of your identity, and aspects of your daily existence. As the astrologer fills in the chart with various symbols and lines, he or she will tell you what it all means. You also can ask specific questions such as, "Will I meet the guy/girl of my dreams this year?" If you're not happy with the answer, you can either choose to accept that life doesn't always go as planned—or decide that astrology really isn't for you, and seek your fate elsewhere.

Get Your Cards Read

Though Tarot cards were developed by Italians in the 1430s, they didn't become linked with fortune-telling until about two and a half centuries later, when French clairvoyants assigned meanings to each of the 56 cards. After shuffling and picking a few cards from the deck, you can have a reader decipher how business, love, money, and spirituality will unfold in your life. Don't let the death card scare you—it often means the death of some aspect of your life, perhaps a bad habit or relationship you've been meaning to kick.

93 Ride a Horse

Y ou've read *Black Beauty*, watched *The Black Stallion*, and bid on a highly collectible Hopalong Cassidy lunch box on eBay. It's safe to say you've got a thing for horses, but have you ever actually ridden one? Roaming hill and dale atop a majestic mare or awesome Appaloosa is a thrilling experience. Humans and horses can form special bonds based on mutual respect and a yearning for freedom. Whether you climb into the saddle just once as part of a family outing or a school trip to a dude ranch, or get more seriously involved with four-legged gamboling (which means frolicking, not gambling), going horseback riding is definitely an experience to be had.

How to Do It

You can get trotting at any number of parks, resorts, and local stables. If you want to pursue equestrian interests more seriously, take a series of classes with a professional trainer. Find a suitable instructor by asking around for references and visiting boarding facilities. Make sure your trainer works with beginners, and be honest about your lack of experience. You'll most likely start out by learning English or Western style riding. Both styles of riding demand a certain posture, careful balance, and a keen understanding of the way horses move, think, and respond to your signals. English, however, is a faster style of riding in which the saddle is smaller, there's no horn to hang on to, and you use both hands to control the reins. Meanwhile, Western is more relaxed with a roomier saddle.

Don't Horse Around

Wear protective gear such as a helmet, boots with a heel, and durable clothing every time you ride. And treat your horse with care. Jerking the reins hurts the horse's mouth (the reins are connected at the corners to a metal piece in its mouth called a bit). Also, quick movements and yelling may spook some horses, so avoid skittish behavior to help ensure your equine does the same. And, of course, it never hurts to use a comforting voice to sweet-talk your horse or feed him carrots and sugar cubes to make him happy.

94 Build a Bonfire

As one of the primal elements—along with earth, air, and water—fire is a mysterious, powerful, and creative yet potentially destructive force of nature. Many cultures celebrate holidays by building fires. In Japan, *bonbi* fires are set to bring back ancestral spirits. On the last Wednesday of the year, Iranians celebrate Chahar Shanbeh Suri by jumping over small fires set in the streets, a custom that is believed to bring good health in the new year. Here in the US, modern-day hippies and artists flock to the Nevada desert for Burning Man, an art show and symbolic fire-burning ritual that happens every summer. Can't make it to any of these places at the moment? Make a simple bonfire with some safety-conscious buddies. Whether basking in its hypnotic glow or circling around it in a tribal dance, you should experience a bonfire at least once in your teen life. It's a great bonding experience with friends and can be really romantic, too.

How to Do It

Gather with a group that includes some outdoorsy people—older family members or buddies who did time with the Scouts. Make sure that your chosen spot is at least 60 feet away from anything that might be flammable—you don't want the fire to spread. Bring plenty of kindling (like twigs and branches) as well as big pieces of wood (up to 6 feet in length and 5 inches around). Wood should be nice and dry, but not rotted. Bring more wood than you think you'll need—it's easy to underestimate the amount necessary to get a good blaze going. Bales of straw work, too. Also bring a shovel, rake, or other tool that you can use to stoke and control the fire. Make sure plenty of water is handy, and, if possible, also bring a fire extinguisher. Gather the kindling in a teepee formation about 4 feet high and around (and don't let the fire grow bigger than 5 feet). Carefully start the fire by lighting the kindling with paper and a lighter or long matches. As the fire begins to burn, add more kindling and wood, graduating to larger pieces. With proper maintenance and some luck, the bonfire should burn for a couple of hours and gradually die out on its own.

Don't Play With Fire

If you are undertaking the task of building a fire, you must also undertake the responsibility of being safe about it. That means:

- Do not build a bonfire on a windy day or evening. If the wind suddenly picks up while the fire is burning, keep a close eye on your flames, and extinguish them immediately if your fire starts to spread in any direction.

- Don't add flammable liquids, fireworks, aerosols, or batteries to a bonfire.

- Don't leave the fire unattended.

- *Never* leave a fire still burning—use water, dirt, and extinguishers to put it all the way out, and scatter the embers so they will not relight.

So many things in life are completely unpredictable, but there's one thing you can bet on without fail: The sun sets in the west and rises in the east. Since the sun sets in the evening, we're often around to watch it sink westward and show off its beauty in a display of vibrant colors. Watching it rise from the east is more challenging since we're usually asleep when it happens. But witnessing a sunrise is an awesome and humbling experience. You'll appreciate the sun like never before and realize just how dependent you are on this almighty star as Earth cycles around it again and again. So forget sleeping in for at least one morning, and get yourself out in time to commune with the early birds to watch the sun soar into the sky and light up the planet.

How to Do It

Check the newspaper or a weather website, like *www.weather.com*, for the exact time of the sunrise. The surest way not to miss it is to stay up all night (on a weekend) and make sure you're positioned in a prime viewing spot at least 30 minutes before it's set to begin. If you don't want to pull an all-nighter, set your alarm for at least an hour before the sunrise is scheduled to start. Plug in the alarm clock far away from your bed so you won't be tempted to hit the Snooze button and miss the magic moment. If possible, you can head to a broad, flat landscape (out in nature, not in a deserted parking lot), where nothing will get in the way of your eastern view, or scramble up to the peak of a small mountain for a bird's-eye view. (Just be sure to bring a buddy and flashlight to help navigate terrain in the dark.) Resist the temptation to snap a ton of pics during the sunrise—they never look nearly as good as the real thing, and you're better off fully experiencing the dawning of the day without worrying if the flash is set to auto. Spend a few moments contemplating the great big world and your place in it as you gaze in wonder at this big star shining from 93 million miles away.

Quite the Sight

Solar eclipses, when the moon blocks sunlight by coming directly between Earth and the sun, are rare but truly spectacular happenings. Read up on their infrequent appearances and far-flung whereabouts, and see if you can be in the right place at the right time to view an obscuring of the sun. (Hint: Do an Internet search for "NASA" and "solar eclipse" for upcoming eclipse dates.) Just don't look directly at the eclipse—view it instead through special glasses made for the occasion. Scientists tell us that the power of the rays can damage our vision.

96 Spend a Day in Silence

Have you heard? Quiet is the new loud. It's time to tone down the nonstop noise of daily life and return, momentarily, to a state of silent grace. By escaping the usual cacophony of voices, car alarms, commercials, and bass-booming hip-hop for 24 hours, you'll realize just how precious the quiet moments really are. Try going an entire day without talking. Do it for yourself as a much-needed break from gabbing with friends and relatives about trivial matters. You'll find that you choose your words more carefully when you begin vocalizing again the next day. You also can remain silent as a political gesture. By not speaking for a whole day, you can call attention to the millions of people worldwide whose restrictive governments, religions, or families prevent them from speaking their minds. Whatever your motivation, button your lip, and see what happens.

How to Do It

Pick a day when you won't be required to speak for school or work. Sundays tend to be slower-paced and more conducive to silence (unless you sing in the church choir). Let your friends and relatives know ahead of time that you'll be unusually quiet, and ask them to respect your silence and privacy throughout the day. Find a relaxing environment—if that's not your house, hunker down in the middle of a tranquil, uninhabited park for the afternoon. Spend the day reading and meditating. Focus on sounds that are usually obscured by noise pollution or your own yakking, such as the chirping of birds or the crashing of waves. Put some headphones on and listen to particularly soothing music such as minimalist Estonian composer Arvo Pärt's delicate piano piece "Für Alina" or French pop duo Air's classic chill-out debut "Moon Safari." If you must communicate with others, use some sort of sign language or write things down.

Retreat Into Silence

Achieve further clarity by participating in a silent retreat at a meditation center or monastery. Retreats can last from one day to two months, with only very short periods of conversation allowed the entire time. Now that's some serious silence.

Average Americans spend much of their time shopping for stuff, making stuff, and getting rid of stuff, but how many people put their stuff in a box to bury it? It may sound weird, but people have been burying time capsules—collections of important items that represent particular people and time periods—for millennia. Have you ever seen a mummy's tomb at the museum? Or that of a saint at a basilica? People used to be buried with all sorts of things that represented who they were and how they spent their time on this planet. But you don't have to bite the dust to gather a few of your favorite possessions and hide them away for posterity. You can dig them up yourself years from now as a reminder of what was most important to you when you were a teenager.

How to Do It

Get together a select group of items that you want to preserve. You can also get a group of friends to join you—it will diversify the collection and bring you all back together later for the unearthing. The items you pick should be important to you, and also uniquely representative of your time and place. Newspapers, magazines, mix CDs with your favorite songs, DVDs, and books (including the one that told you about all of the awesome stuff you should do before finishing high school) are telltale signs of your era, as are photos of yourself, friends, relatives, and people in the news (what will future generations make of Obama or Brangelina?). That letter you wrote to yourself on page 138 can also be a good addition. Put everything in a sturdy, airtight box made of plastic, rubber, or metal, and bury it. Where? If your family owns a home with a backyard, ask if you can dig a hole in an unused plot of dirt. If not, maybe a neighbor or close friend will let you shovel out a portion of their yard. Way out in the woods will work, too. Just be sure not to upset any wildlife or leave a mess. Plant a marker near the buried capsule so you'll remember where to find it, and store a map with the location of your time capsule in a safe place.

Though your teenage years may seem like a real mix of pleasure and pain (and they are), this is still a unique time in your life. Deciding what goes into your time capsule gives you an excuse to examine your present life for a minute and take note of what's in it, for better or for worse. Years later, when you find these things again, you'll be grateful for the prearranged wacky trip down memory lane. And if you never do dig it up yourself, think how cool it would be for someone from the future to find it thousands of years from now and wonder what a Wii remote is.

About the Contributors

Steven Jenkins is a San Francisco-based cultural critic whose writings on film, music, art, and literature appear in national periodicals, exhibition catalogs, and artist monographs. He is the editor of *City Slivers and Fresh Kills: The Films of Gordon Matta-Clark* and *Model Culture: James Casebere, Photographs 1975–1996*.

Erika Stalder is a San Francisco-based writer who has contributed to *Wired* and *Edutopia* magazines and worked with the International Museum of Women to produce the *Imagining Ourselves* anthology. She also wrote Zest Books' *The Date Book: A Teen Girl's Complete Guide to Going Out With Someone New*.

Zest Books would like to extend special thanks to our copy editor, Pennie Rossini, and the following friends who helped us to research this book:

Julia Brashares	Barbara Gatti	Michael Read
Deb Burkman	Pamela King	Eric Rorer
Jonathan Chaet	Rob Larsen	Andie Savard
Arne Johnson	Keith Macklin	Lesley Schwartz
Jorge Kobe	Frances Matthew	Bill Stalder
Erin Garner	Nick and Teresa Morisco	Jo Stalder